RESEARCH FOUNDATION REVIEW 2019

Statement of Purpose

CFA Institute Research Foundation is a not-for-profit organization established to promote the development and dissemination of relevant research for investment practitioners worldwide.

Neither CFA Institute Research Foundation, CFA Institute, nor the publication's editorial staff is responsible for facts and opinions presented in this publication. This publication reflects the views of the author(s) and does not represent the official views of CFA Institute Research Foundation.

CFA®, Chartered Financial Analyst®, and GIPS® are just a few of the trademarks owned by CFA Institute. To view a list of CFA Institute trademarks and the Guide for the Use of CFA Institute Marks, please visit our website at www.cfainstitute.org.

© 2020 CFA Institute Research Foundation. All rights reserved.

No part of this publication may be reproduced, stored in a retrieval system, or transmitted, in any form or by any means, electronic, mechanical, photocopying, recording, or otherwise, without the prior written permission of the copyright holder.

This publication is designed to provide accurate and authoritative information in regard to the subject matter covered. It is sold with the understanding that the publisher is not engaged in rendering legal, accounting, or other professional service. If legal advice or other expert assistance is required, the services of a competent professional should be sought.

Cover credit: Sakda Maprachuab / EyeEm / Getty Images

ISBN 978-1-944960-93-3

CONTENTS

I. THE YEAR IN REVIEW

A Message from Margaret Franklin, CFA 2

Message from the Research Foundation Chair 4

Executive Director's Report 5

Research Directors' Report 9

CFA Institute Research Group Report 14

II. MONOGRAPH SUMMARIES

Investment Governance for Fiduciaries 18
    by Michael E. Drew and Adam N. Walk

Secure Retirement: Connecting Financial Theory and Human Behavior 22
    by Jacques Lussier, CFA

The Productivity Puzzle: Restoring Economic Dynamism 28
    edited by David E. Adler and Laurence B. Siegel

Behavioral Finance: The Second Generation 30
    by Meir Statman

III. LITERATURE REVIEW SUMMARIES

Performance Attribution: History and Progress 34
    by Carl Bacon, CIPM
    summarized by Laurence B. Siegel

IV. BRIEFS SUMMARIES

Relationship Alpha: The Emerging Competitive Advantage
in Wealth Management 38
    by Charlotte B. Beyer

Ten Years After: Reflections on the Global Financial Crisis 40
    by Laurence B. Siegel and Luis Garcia-Feijóo, CFA, CIPM

Tontines: A Practitioner's Guide to Mortality-Pooled Investments 43
    by Richard K. Fullmer, CFA

University Endowments: A Primer 45
    by Richard Franz and Stephan Kranner

A Cash-Flow Focus for Endowments and Trusts 47
  by James P. Garland, CFA

African Capital Markets: Challenges and Opportunities 49
  edited by Heidi Raubenheimer, CFA

V. WORKSHOP FOR THE PRACTITIONER SUMMARIES

The Future of Investment Management 52
  by Ronald N. Kahn

Popularity: A Bridge between Classical and Behavioral Finance 55
  by Roger G. Ibbotson, Thomas M. Idzorek, CFA, Paul D. Kaplan, CFA, and James X. Xiong, CFA

VI. AWARDS AND RECOGNITION

James R. Vertin Award 60
Research Foundation Leadership Circle 63

VII. RECENT PUBLICATIONS

Recent Publications from the Research Foundation Archive 66

I. THE YEAR IN REVIEW

A MESSAGE FROM MARGARET FRANKLIN, CFA

Margaret Franklin, CFA
President and CEO
CFA Institute

It is my great pleasure to welcome you to the CFA Institute Research Foundation Review for 2019.

Although I recently took on the role of president and CEO of CFA Institute, I have long been affiliated with this organization—starting when I earned my charter, of course. Throughout the years, I have always marveled at the convening power and thought leadership emanating from our organization.

It is through the Research Foundation that we deliver thought-provoking and groundbreaking research that helps investment management professionals perform their roles better and stay abreast of the latest developments in our field. I have assumed this role at an interesting point in time for our industry: Our roles are growing more complex, regulations around the world are evolving, and financial technology continues to change the equation.

Some things do not change, however. Fundamental investment analysis remains central to what we do. It is easy to be distracted by the hype around fintech and artificial intelligence (AI), and the future certainly holds great promise for how they can contribute to the investment decision-making process. Nonetheless, we see a future in which technology and AI augment human intelligence, not replace it.

In this world of disruption, one of my main priorities in this role is to ensure that we remain relevant to our members as they address the challenges facing them and their clients. The world is becoming ever more complex, pushing us into new areas where we do not have a ready-made playbook. Climate change, wealth distribution, demographics, and a lower-return environment create formidable challenges as well as new opportunities. The many bodies of work published by the Research Foundation offer important contributions in shaping how we both deliver returns for our investors and grapple with larger societal challenges.

One of the key initiatives currently well underway is our professional learning platform. Our objective is to deliver pertinent and engaging content to members when they want it, how they want it, and where they want it. We believe this will be transformative in the way we serve our members, and we see the work of the Research Foundation as an important contributor to this initiative.

In addition, the efforts of the Research Foundation do not go unnoticed by our societies around the world, providing speakers, books, and other resources to aid them in furthering the professional journey of our members. The Research Foundation is part of our overall research group at CFA Institute, which also includes the *Financial Analysts Journal*, Future of Finance, and *Enterprising Investor*. I am grateful for everything they do.

In closing, I am so proud and honored to be in this role and to be representing CFA Institute and our members to the world. The work of the Research Foundation represents yet another reason for my pride in this organization.

MESSAGE FROM THE RESEARCH FOUNDATION CHAIR

Theodore R. Aronson, CFA
Chair
CFA Institute Research Foundation

It is my privilege to lead the CFA Institute Research Foundation. Together with my colleagues on the Board of Trustees, we govern the mission of the enterprise. The day-to-day operations of the Research Foundation are led by an enthusiastic triumvirate: Bud Haslett, CFA, executive director; Laurence B. Siegel, director of research; and Luis Garcia-Feijóo, CFA, CIPM, associate director of research.

Our mission? Education and enlightenment!

We trace our roots back to 1965, and today the Research Foundation produces publications spanning the entire investment industry—monographs, literature reviews, briefs, and more (https://www.cfainstitute.org/en/research/foundation/publications). Our overarching goal is to publish practitioner-based content at a comprehensive and insightful level. Just peruse these pages to learn of our output over just the past year alone.

As I commented last year, research is the lifeblood of what financial analysts do: Fundamental research reveals security values, market research makes (some!) sense of market behavior, economic research uncovers macroeconomic forces, and quantitative research marries them all. From Ben Graham's "intrinsic value" and "margin of safety" to Robert Shiller's "irrational exuberance," from Paul Samuelson's re-introduction of the "random walk" of security prices to Bill Sharpe's capital asset pricing model—progress advances as a result of research.

The Research Foundation lies at the nexus of all these activities. I am honored to lead a team of volunteer trustees dedicated to our profession. On behalf of those colleagues, thank you for consuming our intellectual output and contributing financially to further the cause. (Every single penny supports those efforts; thus, it is fair to say that voluntary donations to the CFA Institute Research Foundation pay substantial dividends!)

EXECUTIVE DIRECTOR'S REPORT

Bud Haslett, CFA
Executive Director
CFA Institute Research Foundation

The 54th year for the CFA Institute Research Foundation (RF) is now complete, and it was quite a year. As usual, investment publications lead the highlights, with four monographs, a literature review, and six briefs published during the year. Topics for the monographs included governance, retirement, economic productivity, and behavioral finance. In addition, we published literature reviews and briefs on performance attribution, reflections on the great crash, endowments, tontines, and relationships in private wealth. We also added a second edition to our very popular regional publications, this time on the African capital markets in partnership with the African Securities Exchanges Association (ASEA) and some of our member societies in Africa.

Instead of having a number of firsts, as we did in 2018, in 2019 we chose to expand and refine the new projects brought on in 2018. The updated RF website is shaping up nicely, and it is now searchable by year and by type of product (e.g., multimedia audio and video). The new accounting system is close to being fully optimized, providing valuable information for our future decision making. We also expanded the RF translation program to six languages, adding Arabic and Japanese versions of selected RF content alongside Chinese, French, Portuguese, and Spanish versions. These translations—as well as the growing volume of global RF content—highlight the truly global nature of the Research Foundation.

The year was not without its new projects, however, as 2019 saw a digitization program that will make available over 30 previously unavailable pieces of RF content. In addition, the Research Foundation introduced new interactive content sites for the *Research Foundation Review 2018* and *African Capital Markets* that are visually stunning. We look forward to producing many more of these easy-to-navigate sites in the future. Also, RF content on trading and exchange-traded funds will be added to the upcoming CFA exam curriculum, and other RF content is being reviewed for future inclusion.

Producing great content is not enough if no one reads it, so during 2019, the Research Foundation embarked on an expanded social media program to increase content usage. In addition to the $10,000 a month of free search advertising provided by the Google Grants program, we expanded our LinkedIn and Twitter presence substantially during the year. If you have not done so already, please take a moment to follow us on these two important platforms.

On a different note, we chose to shutter our popular Research Foundation Society Award in its eighth year because it is being replaced by a research award representing the entire research group (the Research Foundation, *Financial Analysts Journal*, Future of Finance, and *Enterprising Investor*). We extend our thanks to the more than 30 CFA Institute member societies that won the award over the years and assure them that their projects and activities will live on in future RF events and content.

In May 2019, RF chair Ted Aronson moderated the 18th Research Foundation Workshop for the Practitioner held during the CFA Institute Annual Conference in London. This year's lineup was a blockbuster, featuring BlackRock's Ronald Kahn discussing his monograph *The Future of Investment Management* and Yale's Roger Ibbotson discussing his monograph on popularity. Both authors took time after their presentation to sign books for attendees and conducted multi-stop presentations at various member societies in the Europe, Middle East, and Africa (EMEA) region. Copies of their books and videos of their presentations are available at https://www.cfainstitute.org/en/research/foundation for your learning enjoyment. And in May 2020, make sure to check out the 19th RF Workshop, featuring Meir Statman and Pedro Matos discussing behavioral finance and environmental, social, and governance concerns at the CFA Institute Annual Conference in Atlanta.

Unfortunately, a sad note surrounded the 2019 Vertin Award as winner John Bogle passed away soon after learning of his selection for the award. We were pleased to know that Jack was delighted to receive the award, and his son John Bogle, Jr., CFA, accepted the Vertin Award in his father's honor at the CFA Society Boston Annual Meeting. All in attendance at the ceremony were moved by John Jr.'s heartfelt speech, with current CFA Institute chair and RF board member Diane Nordin, CFA, making the presentation. We thank Jack for making tremendous contributions to the field of investment management and recognize he will be greatly missed by all who knew him as well as all in the investment business.

2019 Vertin Award winner John Bogle with son John Bogle, Jr.

The Research Foundation once again had the honor of working with numerous global CFA Institute member societies during 2019. This initiative is incredibly important for the Research Foundation: We provide complimentary books and speakers for dozens upon dozens of society events as well as partner with the societies to bring important investment content to the marketplace. We also had the honor of being hosted by CFA Society Victoria and CFA Society Emirates for our 2019 June and November board meetings, respectively. These meetings are critical in developing the strategical guidance for the future path of the Research Foundation. They also feature a great opportunity for the RF board to meet and mingle with society leaders and members during the joint social events held on the evening between the two-day board meeting.

Speaking of the RF board, we would like to take a moment to thank Diane Lambert, George Hoguet, CFA, and past RF chair Jeff Bailey, CFA, for their multi-year commitment to the Research Foundation and welcome new board members Lotta Moberg, CFA, Dave Uduanu, CFA, and Roger Ibbotson to the 2020 RF board. We would also like to congratulate Joanne Hill for her new role as vice chair and wish her luck when she assumes the RF chair next year.

As the Research Foundation completes yet another year, we take this opportunity to thank the many dozens of people responsible for its operation. From the great staff and leadership at CFA Institute to the excellent strategic guidance provided by the RF board to the financial contributions by CFA Institute and the many thousands of members and others who each year donate to the Research Foundation, we could not do it without you. To our research directors Laurence B. Siegel and Luis Garcia-Feijóo, CFA, CIPM; CFA Institute Research Group leader Rhodri Preece, CFA; project manager Jessica Lawson; and the dozens of talented authors writing RF content: We could not do it without you. And finally, to the tens of thousands of people who have, over the years, read our content and gained valuable knowledge from it, we thank you.

2018–2019 CFA Institute Research Foundation Board members at board meeting in Victoria, British Columbia.

2019–2020 CFA Institute Research Foundation board members at board meeting in Abu Dhabi, United Arab Emirates.

As I approach the latter years of my career in the investment industry, it is with the utmost honor that I serve as executive director of this esteemed organization. I pledge to dedicate the remaining years of my career to continuing to make the Research Foundation prosper, and I very much look forward to announcing in 2020 a new RF project that will greatly expand our value and offerings to all CFA Institute members and others in the investment community. Many thanks for the privilege.

RESEARCH DIRECTORS' REPORT

Laurence B. Siegel
Gary P. Brinson Director of Research
CFA Institute Research Foundation

Luis Garcia-Feijóo, CFA, CIPM
Associate Research Director
Florida Atlantic University

In 2019, the Research Foundation disseminated four research monographs, a literature review, and six briefs.

Research Monographs

Beneficiaries First: Guidance for Fiduciaries

In *Investment Governance for Fiduciaries*, Michael Drew and Adam Walk propose a framework for the effective use of resources by the fiduciary (the agent) in addressing an underlying investment challenge affecting the beneficiary (the principal). Their framework emphasizes process over financial prowess. The focus is on investment governance expertise, not investment expertise, recognizing that achieving investment objectives is the reason the fiduciary relationship exists in the first place. Their framework involves a circular process with the following steps: Objective, Policy, Execute and Resource, Implement, and Superintend (OPERIS). The authors' work follows up on the Research Foundation's (RF's) previous forays into trustee education, including *A Primer for Investment Trustees: Understanding Investment Committee Responsibilities* (2017) by Jeffrey V. Bailey, CFA, and Thomas M. Richards, CFA.

Engineering a Secure Retirement

William Sharpe said that retirement finance was the toughest engineering problem he had ever worked on. It is difficult to figure out how much to save because (1) you do not know how long you are going to live, (2) you do not know how much money you will need in each year you survive after retirement, (3) you do not know what return you will make on your investments, and (4) if you *did* know how much you needed to save, you would probably have a heart attack and die (solving the first problem expeditiously).

Jacques Lussier's *Secure Retirement: Connecting Financial Theory and Human Behavior* is an engineer's approach to solving these problems. He uses a series of Monte Carlo simulations to show the impact of each important decision on retirement outcomes. He also shows the impact of combined decisions (say, the decision to save more and invest more aggressively), which is a neat trick made possible by Monte Carlo technology.

Lussier's analytics are not the only way to address retirement. His monograph is only one in an extensive series of RF works on this general topic. We have, over the years, also published three conference proceedings monographs on retirement organized by Zvi Bodie (2007, 2009, 2012); a literature review on *Longevity Risk and Retirement Income Planning* (2015); Moshe Milevsky's 2013 monograph on life annuities; the 2007 monograph *Lifetime Financial Advice: Human Capital, Asset Allocation, and Insurance*, by Roger Ibbotson and three coauthors; and, this year, a brief on tontines (described subsequently).

The Great Headache

The Great Recession did not happen very long ago, but economic conditions have improved. But have they improved at a rate one would expect in a bounce back from the depression-like conditions of 2007–2009? Almost all economists would say no. Something is missing.

In *The Productivity Puzzle: Restoring Economic Dynamism*, David Adler and Laurence Siegel, who edited this collection of readings, focus on the slow growth of productivity. The authors of the articles in the monograph (many of whom spoke at a 2017 conference on the topic) present viewpoints that are all over the map. Two unifying themes, however, are particularly worth mentioning: (1) The idea that the age of great technological advancement is over—that today's economy is as good as it is going to get—is absurd. Everyone who has prophesied that "everything worth inventing has already been invented" has turned out to be laughably wrong and will continue to be. (2) Nevertheless, technological change, including change that results in large advancements in standards of living, comes in waves. We may need to wait for another great wave of innovation to see the kind of long-term growth we have come to expect.

The authors suggest various solutions, including better education, apprenticeship programs, infrastructure spending, and increases in basic scientific research.

On Behavioral Finance and Classical Finance

In his monograph *Behavioral Finance: The Second Generation*, Meir Statman, a pioneer in behavioral thinking about finance, helps to build a bridge between the two sides. He sets forth a "Behavioral Finance 2.0" that describes people as neither rational (the classical assumption) nor irrational (the idea behind BF 1.0) but *normal*.

In Statman's words, normal people "want three kinds of benefits—utilitarian, expressive, and emotional—from all activities, products, and services, including financial activities, products, and services." It is not irrational to want these benefits, so normal people's wants are consistent with the classical economist's assumption that people are utility maximizers. Statman's BF 2.0 offers a different and more complete perspective on what people value—that is, on what they are maximizing when they seek to increase their utility.

For example, those who are underperforming may well be satisfying some component of their utility function other than maximizing return subject to a concern about risk. One does not have to beat the S&P 500 Index, or any other index, to be a successful investor by one's own lights.

Literature Review

How Performance Attribution Evolved

Carl Bacon, CIPM, provides an authoritative literature review on performance attribution from a historical viewpoint. It is entitled "Performance Attribution: History and Progress." He starts by explaining what performance attribution is and why it is useful. He reviews the early contributions of the Bank Administration Institute, Peter Dietz, and the group surrounding Gary Brinson and then moves to more modern innovations. The history is valuable in helping the reader to understand how performance attribution evolved from a simple attempt to measure returns into a complex science that has its own journal, an army of sophisticated practitioners, and a large population of clients with varying needs.

Briefs

Money Doctors

In Charlotte Beyer's brief, *Relationship Alpha: The Emerging Competitive Advantage in Wealth Management*, she suggests that a private wealth advisor must develop a long-term relationship with his or her client in order to better determine the client's goals (risk aversion and investment objective), the best course of action and possible hurdles (e.g., taxes), and the level of financial sophistication expected at client meetings. The relationship must also help the client better understand the advisor's capabilities and limitations. In short, the advisor must become a "money doctor" (to borrow a term from a related academic research piece published in the *Journal of Finance*).[1]

A Somewhat Unhappy Anniversary

We still do not know exactly what went wrong in the global economy and financial markets between the summer of 2007 and the spring of 2009. There are many guilty parties. Whatever the proximate cause, the meltdown was spectacularly awful. No living market participant had ever seen anything like it.

To address this fiasco, New York University and the *Annual Review of Financial Economics* convened a group of central bankers and economic researchers to reflect on the causes, events, and long-run outcomes of the Global Financial Crisis. This event took place around the 10th anniversary of the crisis, hence the title of the Research Foundation's brief based on the conference, *Ten Years After: Reflections on the Global Financial Crisis*.

The highlight was the central banker roundtable, which featured Stanley Fischer as moderator(!) and Ben Bernanke, Lord Mervyn King, and Jean-Claude Trichet as the principal speakers. All four were heads of central banks at the time of the crisis.[2] Their comments, as well as those of the many other economists who participated in the conference, are available on video at the RF website as well as in the brief.

---

[1] Nicola Gennaioli, Andrei Shleifer, and Robert Vishny, "Money Doctors," *Journal of Finance* 70 (February 2015): 91–114.

[2] Respectively, in Israel, the United States, the United Kingdom and at the European Central Bank.

Tontines: Betting on a Long Life

One of the oddest missing links in the financial system is the absence of a secure, transparent, and low-cost mechanism for investors planning for retirement to insure against longevity risk. The mirror image of mortality risk (the risk of dying), longevity risk is the risk of outliving one's money. Life annuities are a step in the right direction, but most are overpriced and opaque as to both costs and benefits.

A better potential solution to this problem is right in front of our faces. In *Tontines: A Practitioner's Guide to Mortality-Pooled Investments*, Richard K. Fullmer, CFA, reaches back in time to an invention by Lorenzo de Tonti, a 17th-century Italian banker (hence the name "tontine"). A group of people pool their assets so that as each one dies, the surviving group members share the remainder.

Fullmer's RF brief develops the tontine idea into a full-fledged suite of hypothetical financial products. He shows the math behind a design that would allow participants of different ages and/or life expectancies to enter a tontine pool at actuarially fair prices. This approach would make the formation of large, anonymous pools practical.

Endowment Funds: Providing Perpetual Support for Education

Endowment funds play a central role in supporting the long-term survival and smooth operations of colleges and universities, but donations and market performance fluctuate, making sound management imperative. In this context, Richard Franz and Stephan Kranner's brief, *University Endowments: A Primer*, offers an excellent overview of both how endowments work and how they *should* work. Assets under management at college and university endowments in the United States totaled approximately $570 billion as of June 2017.

Endowments have some unique features. Their time horizon is not merely long term; it is perpetual, giving them an advantage in earning an illiquidity premium. But illiquidity can also pose a risk, because schools typically have the greatest need of liquidity for spending when it is least available. Franz and Kranner cover these and other important issues in endowment management.

Setting Spending Rates for Endowment Funds and Similar Institutions

Setting spending rates for individuals with a limited but unknown length of life is difficult because of longevity risk: We do not know how long the money needs to last. But why does setting spending rates for perpetual endowment funds and for other long-lived trusts seem equally hard? Universities, foundations, and families have wrestled with this problem seemingly forever and have come up with a variety of conflicting answers:

- Spend only investment "income."

- Spend income and realized but not unrealized capital gains.

- Spend an amount each year that is fixed in constant dollars (i.e., ratchet up spending each year by the inflation rate).

- Spend a fixed percentage of the market value of the assets each year.

- Decide how much to spend each year.

The second-to-last answer, a fixed percentage of market value (or some variant, such as a fixed percentage of a rolling three-year average of market values), is currently in favor. The Ford Foundation advocated this method in an influential 1969 report, and the approach is still with us a half-century later. But the question remains open.

Although "income" can be a legal or accounting concept, the word also has an economic meaning: namely, what you can consume in a given period without being worse off at the end of the period (in real terms) than at the beginning, assuming no change in market valuations. In the RF brief *A Cash-Flow Focus for Endowments and Trusts*, James Garland, CFA, builds on this concept to define the "fecundity" of an asset in exactly that way. (Fecundity, in biology, is the fertility of an organism per unit of time—high for rabbits, low for elephants.) For bonds, fecundity is yield, minus an allowance for defaults if the bond is risky; for stocks, it is a concept akin to free cash flow, representing the economic profit of the company.

A spending rule tied to fecundity (and ignoring market values) will give very different results from the currently popular rule specifying a percentage of market value. It will increase spending, relative to the market-value rule, when markets are cheap and will decrease it when markets are expensive. It will also produce a smoother spending path. Each institution or individual will have to decide which spending rule makes the most sense in that institution's or individual's particular situation.

African Local Capital Markets: Past, Present, and Future

Demographic trends and economic growth expectations indicate that future investment opportunities with attractive risk–return profiles will likely come from outside developed markets. In particular, African markets are regarded with promise. They are, however, not a unitary construct. For example, MSCI classifies South Africa and Egypt as emerging; Kenya, Mauritius, Morocco, Nigeria, Tunisia, and the countries in the West African Economic and Monetary Union as frontier; and Botswana and Zimbabwe as neither emerging nor frontier, although they have their own standalone market indices. Some countries export oil and gas; others, precious metals and minerals or coffee; and yet others, non-commodities such as textiles. Furthermore, sovereign and corporate bond markets, as well as exchange-traded funds, need to be understood in these countries.

The brief *African Capital Markets: Challenges and Opportunities*, produced in collaboration with the African Securities Exchanges Association (ASEA), addresses these issues for South Africa, Namibia, Botswana, Zimbabwe, Mauritius, Kenya, Tanzania, Uganda, Rwanda, Nigeria, Ghana, Egypt, and Morocco and presents aggregate data on the size and liquidity of the equity and fixed-income markets in these countries.

CFA INSTITUTE RESEARCH GROUP REPORT

Rhodri Preece, CFA
Senior Head, Industry Research
CFA Institute

The CFA Institute Research Foundation complements the wider activities of the research division of CFA Institute, which also comprises journal publications (*Financial Analysts Journal* and *CFA Digest*), the Future of Finance initiative, and the *Enterprising Investor* blog.

Our aim is to develop research relevant to the investment management industry that advances knowledge, understanding, and professionalism of CFA Institute members, practitioners, and industry leaders.

To achieve this goal, we produce a spectrum of research across our publications platforms, providing investment professionals with a balance of rigorous in-depth research, forward-looking thought leadership content, applied investment insights, and commentary on trending investment topics.

In addition to the work accomplished by the Research Foundation encapsulated in this review, the research group's activities in 2019 included the publication of several reports and outreach with industry stakeholders to advance our thought leadership agenda, among other initiatives.

In Future of Finance, our flagship publication in 2019 was "Investment Professional of the Future," which analyzes individual roles, skills, and organizational cultures in the investment profession. It examines how technological disruption and other trends will shape investment jobs and the structure of investment teams in the future. This research builds on earlier work that examined the drivers of change in the investment industry and their implications for investment firms. The research was launched in May 2019 and has attracted more than 10,000 downloads to date, in addition to leading to numerous industry engagements.

The emergence of artificial intelligence (AI) in the investment industry has captured much attention among investment professionals. To help individuals and firms better make sense of the potential use cases, opportunities, and hurdles to successfully deploying AI technologies, we published "AI Pioneers in Investment Management" in September 2019. The report contains a collection of case studies with firms from across the globe that illustrate where and how to use AI and big data in investment processes.

In journal publications, we maintained our regular publishing cycle of high-quality research articles. The *Financial Analysts Journal*, our flagship publication, continues to experience growth in article submissions and citations, and our "impact factor"—an academic measure of article quality based on citations—rose from 1.413 to 1.816 over the year. The Graham and Dodd Award for 2019, which recognizes excellence in research and financial writing in the *Financial Analysts Journal*, was given to Jason Hsu, Vitali Kalesnik, and Engin Kose for their article "What Is Quality?," which examines the "quality" factor and the robustness of different measures that are associated with a return premium. Looking ahead, the *Financial Analysts Journal* will celebrate its 75th anniversary in 2020, which will be marked with several activities and special articles.

Environmental, social, and governance (ESG) considerations continue to feature in industry debates and in the development of investment strategies and products. To support high-quality research on ESG issues and the expansion of the body of knowledge, CFA Institute has participated in two academic research networks: The Global Research Alliance for Sustainable Finance and Investment (GRASFI), through which the *Financial Analysts Journal* sponsored two paper prizes in 2019, and the Principles for Responsible Investment (PRI) academic network advisory committee. In addition, in December 2019, we published "Sustainable, Responsible, and Impact Investing and Islamic Finance: Similarities and Differences." The research provides an entry point for investment professionals to explore Islamic finance and socially responsible investing approaches, highlighting the ethical orientation of both. ESG issues will continue to feature in our research agenda in 2020.

Our research blog platform, *Enterprising Investor*, is a forum for provocative analysis of current issues in finance and investing. Over the course of 2019, *Enterprising Investor* experienced growth in authors and subscribers. We attracted an average of more than 90,000 visitors each month, receiving a total of more than 1.3 million article views. Views have grown by approximately 50% year on year (at the time of writing).

The Research Foundation is an integral part of the wider research offering of CFA Institute, and the publication of this review provides a perfect companion to the other reports and activities highlighted herein. We hope you find the material insightful and thought provoking.

II. MONOGRAPH SUMMARIES

INVESTMENT GOVERNANCE FOR FIDUCIARIES

by Michael E. Drew and Adam N. Walk

Governance is a word that is increasingly heard and read in modern times, be it corporate governance, global governance, or investment governance. Investment governance, the central concern of this modest volume, refers to the effective employment of resources—people, policies, processes, and systems—by an individual or governing body (the fiduciary or agent) seeking to fulfill its fiduciary duty to a principal (or beneficiary) in addressing an underlying investment challenge.

Effective investment governance is an enabler of good stewardship, and for this reason it should, in our view, be of interest to all fiduciaries, no matter the size of the pool of assets or the nature of the beneficiaries. To emphasize the importance of effective investment governance and to demonstrate its flexibility across organization types, we consider our investment governance process within three contexts: defined contribution (DC) plans, defined benefit (DB) plans, and endowments and foundations (E&Fs).

Since the financial crisis of 2007–2008, the financial sector's place in the economy and its methods and ethics have (rightly, in many cases) been under scrutiny. Coupled with this theme, the task of investment governance is of increasing importance due to the sheer weight of money, the retirement savings gap, demographic trends, regulation and activism, and rising standards of behavior based on higher expectations from those fiduciaries serve. These trends are at the same time related and self-reinforcing.

Having explored the why of investment governance, we dedicate the remainder of the book to the question of how to bring it to bear as an essential component of good fiduciary practice. At this point, the reader might expect investment professionals to launch into a discussion about an investment process focused on the best way to capture returns. We resist this temptation. Instead, we contend that achieving outcomes on behalf of beneficiaries is as much about managing risks as it is about capturing returns—and we mean "risks" broadly construed, not just fluctuations in asset values.

The metaphor we use for this investment governance process thus emphasizes the defensive aspects of solving the investment challenge, especially defending the beneficiary from risk events and/or uncompensated risks (as well as capturing returns). Given the uncertainty involved in investment decision making, the fiduciary investor is left to rely on a robust process.

To underscore the idea of defense, we have adopted a Latin word used to describe field defenses, *operis*, as the way to remember the key steps of our investment process. OPERIS spells out the steps in the process— Objective, Policy, Execute and Resource, Implement, Superintend—and we devote the remainder of this volume to exploring the how of investment governance with reference to our three organizational contexts: DC plans, DB plans, and E&Fs.

By the end of the book, we hope it will be clear to the reader that the individual fiduciary and the governing body to which the fiduciary is appointed each face a difficult task. How might one both represent the interests of beneficiaries and make complex investment decisions in the presence of uncertainty and competing interests? In such a context, we submit that a high probability of success is perhaps the best that can be hoped for.

We set out to provide fiduciaries with some ideas that might help them increase the probability of success. Almost all our suggestions point to the need for a good process that is defensible, repeatable, and documented and that can be used as evidence of diligence in fulfilling the role of fiduciary. Applied diligently by the fiduciary body through time, this process seeks to maximize the probability of achieving the objectives set on behalf of beneficiaries.

In making the case for good process, we offer a high-level outline of the process we use when consulting and counseling our fiduciary clients. We find that this process provides a nearly universal blueprint for addressing the issues investors face, noting that the investment challenge—and the investment policy statement that flows from it—can vary widely depending on the context and/or the nature of the beneficiary. We are the first to emphasize that we are not advocating our process as the only possible path to defensible fiduciary practice. Instead, we contend that it is more important to have a process than to necessarily have this process.

This book is the fruit of the last 25 years or so of professional experience across industry and academia, during which we have worked—mostly with each other—on matters of investment governance. Our professional collaboration began when we worked as the senior investment governance officers of a pension fund that offered both DB and DC plans and where the investment function was substantially delegated to external parties (some of which were related). The investment governance ecosystem in which this fund existed was formative in our views on the subject. We began as staff acting as gatekeepers for lay fiduciaries, faced with the best (and worst) the industry has to offer during the best and worst of times (including the global financial crisis).

Now, as independent consultants and fiduciaries, we see the same issues from a slightly different perspective. Some of our views have been confirmed, others challenged. What has become patently obvious to us is that good process has common elements and (near) universal application irrespective of the fiduciary role and the underlying investment challenge.

A book about investment governance for fiduciaries is important because the task they face is of increasing importance the world over. Fiduciaries are trusted with being stewards of other people's money, money that has been set aside for important societal purposes, be that the retirement savings of thousands of workers, the wealth of nations, or the legacy and good works of a charity.

The intent of this book is thus to share with fiduciaries ideas that may help them fulfil their duties to beneficiaries (and other stakeholders). Asset consultants and investment managers may find it useful in establishing their credibility among, and pitching their services to, fiduciaries. What is sure is that this book has been written for fiduciaries, who, in our experience, take seriously the underappreciated role for which they are appointed (often on a pro bono basis). While some of the words will grate on some industry players, we have challenged the industry to follow the advice of Charles D. Ellis, CFA, in his well-known *Financial Analysts Journal* paper "The Winners' Game" (2011, vol. 67, no. 4): "Prioritize the *values* of the profession (i.e., serve those it should be serving) over the *economics* [original emphasis] of the business (its own commercial interests)."

We trust that this book contributes to raising the standards of fiduciary practice among stewards of wealth.

The publication can be found at
https://www.cfainstitute.org/en/research/foundation/2019/investment-governance-for-fiduciaries

Use your mobile device to scan the QR code to go straight to the webpage.

SECURE RETIREMENT: CONNECTING FINANCIAL THEORY AND HUMAN BEHAVIOR

by Jacques Lussier, CFA

The Context

Investors fear return uncertainty and drawdowns associated with owning relatively risky asset classes, such as equity. The fact that greater risk is associated with greater expected return does not preclude the possibility that realized returns may be far less than a low-risk asset could provide, even with horizons as long as 5 to 10 years. Fear prompts the average investor to sometimes act against his own best interest. Therefore, the average investor's portfolio often underperforms a static benchmark, even before fees. The average investor tends to increase allocation to riskier assets after the market has already significantly risen and decrease allocation after a significant decline.

Given that financial planning in the context of retirement is a multidecade endeavor that can last 50 years or more, investors face an additional challenge. Financial planners cannot be concerned solely with "managing" the behavior of investors facing short-term return uncertainty, which remains an important challenge, but must also be concerned with how to address longer-term uncertainties. For example, there is significant uncertainty about the assumption for long-term expected returns, real as well as nominal. Some lucky investors may accumulate much of their wealth before retirement during an exceptionally strong bull market (e.g., 1982 to 2000), whereas less fortunate investors may have been planning to retire in 2008 or early 2009, just after the most dramatic global liquidity crisis since the Great Depression and a significant decline in interest rates. Moreover, average expected returns represent only part of the story. Some investors may have recorded above-average returns at a time when their accumulated wealth was already significant, whereas others may have recorded above-average returns when their accumulated wealth was low. The implication of the interactions among savings patterns (in accumulation), withdrawal patterns (in decumulation), and timing of above- and below-average portfolio returns is important to understand, particularly with respect to how the interactions should affect the allocation policy.

Furthermore, investors face significant risks in the transition period—say, the last 5 to 10 years—from accumulation to decumulation. Considering the uncertainty in long-term expected returns, patterns of returns, and patterns of savings, it is unlikely that a financial plan established when an individual is 30 years old can remain static thereafter. The plan must be revaluated periodically, which requires an effective feedback mechanism or tool. The investor has many more options available before retirement, however, although some may not necessarily be pleasant. In the event of lower than expected accumulated wealth, the investor could decide to save more, postpone retirement, and/or adjust retirement plans. These options may be unavailable or may be harder to implement once the decision to retire has been made. The investor must implement a transition strategy that reduces the likelihood and/or significance of the unplanned adjustments that may be necessary as the targeted or desired retirement date draws near.

In addition, longevity remains uncertain, and retirement plans often are based on expected longevity. Even though the median life expectancy for a 65-year-old individual in the United States is 83.3 years for men and 85.9 years for women, a significant percentage of people will live past age 90. Furthermore, as someone ages, the older she is expected to live. A dynamic issue, life expectancy becomes even more complicated in the context of a couple—one or both individuals could live a very long time. This possibility should also influence the allocation policy over time and the potential need for longevity insurance.

Finally, governments in many countries have implemented policies and programs to support the retirement effort. The most important program in the United States is Social Security, but its purpose is to provide only a minimum level of inflation-adjusted income, not to sustain the standard of living that an individual had before retirement. Other programs seek to encourage savings and facilitate wealth accumulation, such as 401(k)s, traditional and Roth IRAs (Registered Retirement Savings Plans and Tax-Free Savings Accounts in Canada), and health savings accounts (HSAs). Most investors, however, underestimate the savings effort required to maintain the standard of living to which they are accustomed, cannot implement a comprehensive and coherent adaptive retirement plan, cannot optimize across all relevant parameters, and lack access to the feedback mechanism needed to make the appropriate adjustments over time.

Secure Retirement and Other Literature

Many books on retirement planning have been published in recent years. Almost exclusively, they cover general issues of retirement preparedness, public policy, asset allocation and asset location principles, and lifestyle recommendations. These books provide useful guidelines and simple investment rules of thumb. Recommendations are often based on relatively simple analytics, sometimes illustrated in a single-period context, and/or are supported by referring to more in-depth studies published in academic journals or business research. For example, CFA Institute published a comprehensive literature review titled *Longevity Risk and Retirement Income Planning*,[3] which aggregates much of the relevant literature.

Currently, however, no book links the academic and business research on the most relevant dimensions of retirement planning—such as risk in accumulation and decumulation, longevity risk, longevity products, asset allocation, taxation, and measures of utility—and tests this research within an integrated and realistic empirical framework. Furthermore, some aspects of retirement planning have been insufficiently researched. For example, although how to better manage risk in decumulation is currently a focus of interest, the nature of risk in accumulation and how it should affect allocation policy are still not well understood by most investors.

Improving retirement planning is therefore a complex challenge that requires a comprehensive and integrated theoretical and empirical effort. As Robert Merton said in a 2017 interview, "The retirement problem is a global problem. The good news is, finance science can be used to solve it. Design things on finance principles, rather than institutionally.... If you design on financial principles, it will work everywhere in the world."[4] Designing a solution to the retirement problem based on financial principles is the goal of *Secure Retirement*. Although written in the context of US (and, at times, Canadian) investors, its principles are universal. *Secure Retirement* is written not only for sophisticated investors and financial advisers but also for those interested in creating more informationally efficient web-based retirement platforms. Its findings can be applied to all investors, although the investments of individuals with super-high net worth require greater complexity with respect to assets and asset classes, insurance products, taxation, and legal framework.

The Content

The material of *Secure Retirement* is concentrated in seven core chapters, Chapters 2 to 8. The introductory chapter (Chapter 1) frames the main issues and the scope of this book. The concluding chapter (Chapter 9) explores improvements that should eventually be integrated into this effort but would require new research and highly advanced quantitative methodologies, such as machine-learning models and algorithms.

---

[3]Patrick J. Collins, Huy D. Lam, and Josh Stampfli, *Longevity Risk and Retirement Income Planning* (Charlottesville, VA: CFA Institute Research Foundation, 2015).

[4]Robert C. Merton, Fiduciary Investors Symposium at the Massachusetts Institute of Technology (2017).

Secure Retirement relies on a building-block approach. Most arguments are supported in the following way:

- A logical argument and its expected consequence are presented.

- The argument is supported using scenario analyses.

- The argument is further supported in the context of a simulation environment.

Chapter 2 explains the relevant dimensions of retirement planning in the absence of uncertainty. Chapters 3, 4, and 5 increase our understanding of risk in the context of accumulation (Chapter 3), decumulation (Chapter 4), and the transition between these periods (Chapter 5). They also discuss what allocation strategies and tools are appropriate in each context, incorporating the effects of Social Security and annuities. Chapter 6 discusses the different methodological processes that can be used to apply and calibrate a comprehensive retirement approach that considers all three phases of the retirement process. It also presents the different measures of utility and satisfaction that may be appropriate in different contexts, such as when investors have excess wealth and intend to use this wealth for a specific purpose. One such measure is the percentage of PIO (preferred income objective) target, which measures the average percentage of the preferred inflation-adjusted retirement income target expected to be achieved across all scenarios and over time. This measure uses adjusted mortality assumptions to account for the concerns of retirees who may live much longer than the median mortality age. *Secure Retirement* emphasizes sustained retirement income rather than wealth accumulation.

Up to Chapter 6, the retirement framework is designed around a simple context characterized by few asset classes and no taxation. Chapter 7 adds broader considerations related to asset allocation and choice of asset classes, taxation and asset location, life insurance, the relevance of variable annuity products, the appropriate income replacement ratio, the role of reverse mortgages, the choice of mortality assumptions, and the complexity of a household.

Finally, Chapter 8 presents a fairly comprehensive model of retirement planning and applies it to our prototype investor, named John. An integrated simulation engine was specifically designed for this chapter. Chapter 8 illustrates how successive improvements made to our framework change John's expected retirement income distribution and the expected utility derived from consumption (such as his percentage of PIO target). The model is applied when John is 30 years old and then again when he is only 5 years from retirement. In a real-life context, the model should likely be reapplied periodically, perhaps yearly, especially if circumstances (income, health, financial conditions, and so on) change dramatically.

Secure Retirement is not about active management of specific asset classes. Although we have conducted research on the effect of using factor-investing approaches to modify the distribution of equity returns (but not the expected return), the book's emphasis remains on risk management and long-term financial planning.

Some Major Observations

Secure Retirement covers too many aspects to properly address here. Some important observations can be made, however. Consider the following five aspects.

First, the effect of return volatility on cumulative wealth in the context of periodic savings contributions during the accumulation phase differs greatly from its effect in the context of static wealth (implying no new savings contribution). Volatility can enhance the expectation of cumulative wealth and improve its expected distribution when the current level of wealth is small relative to the present value of future savings contributions. This dynamic can lead to higher portfolio returns even in a low market return environment. Therefore, without increasing expected downside risk, volatility provides support for very high levels of equity exposure for a period that can extend up to 15 years before retirement.

Second, we can use our understanding of risk in the context of accumulation to derive more-effective allocation glide paths between higher- and lower-risk asset classes. In addition, our analyses show that a dynamic allocation strategy—such as that proposed by Giron, Martellini, Milhau, Mulvey, and Suri (2018), inspired by the constant proportion portfolio insurance (CPPI) approach—can significantly reduce yearly drawdowns without unfavorably affecting the distribution of expected retirement income.[5] Furthermore, we show that the portfolio turnover resulting from the implementation of their approach, an issue ignored in their original research, can be significantly reduced.

Third, our research does not support the frequent argument that purchasing single-premium annuities in a low interest rate environment is inadvisable. We found that incorporating an annuity component allows us to maintain a higher equity allocation in the remaining liquid asset portfolio. We do not advise substituting annuities for equity or even for a balanced portfolio, but they may be substituted for a portion of the fixed-income component. This approach considerably alleviates the argument against annuities in a low interest rate environment even though their expected duration is longer than that of most fixed-income portfolios. In fact, an annuity strategy should be implemented gradually because a market crisis (leading simultaneously to lower yields and low equity prices) occurring in the final years leading to retirement can significantly affect this strategy's efficiency.

Fourth, we examined the question of asset location—that is, which assets should be placed in which type of accounts according to their respective tax status. Should higher expected return assets, taxed at a lower rate than other assets, be allocated to the taxable account in priority or to the tax-deferred/tax-exempt accounts? Those advisers who recommend allocating higher expected return assets first to tax-deferred/tax-exempt accounts support their argument through the return-compounding benefits of higher expected return assets. Those who recommend allocating these assets to the taxable account argue that although taxation lowers net expected returns, it also reduces risk; in addition, the tax rate

---
[5]Kevin Giron, Lionel Martellini, Vincent Milhau, John Mulvey, and Anil Suri, "Applying Goal-Based Investing Principles to the Retirement Problem" (EDHEC-Risk Institute, May 2018).

applied to interest income is higher than the rate applied to equity (dividends and capital gains). Our research shows the appropriate answer is more subtle than either recommendation but generally supports allocating riskier assets first to tax-deferred/tax-exempt accounts at long investment horizons.

Finally, overall simulation results obtained in a comprehensive setting show that coherent and disciplined allocation and risk management processes can significantly enhance investors' well-being. Consider the case of our prototype investor, John. What started as a percentage of PIO target of 64.9% for the bottom half of all scenarios generated when John was 30 years old—the top half of all scenarios scored close to 100%—ended with a score of 90.1% when John reached the age of 60 and all efficiency improvements were implemented. Furthermore, the worst expected yearly drawdowns over the plan's lifetime were reduced by 30%.

Our work shows that a well-designed financial planning tool is essential to support the work of investors and financial planners. The challenge is simply too complex to be handled by simple rules of thumb, current generic robo-advisers, or simple Excel spreadsheets. Eventually, implementing machine-learning algorithms to improve longevity assumptions and asset allocation decisions will further improve the results.

The publication can be found at
https://www.cfainstitute.org/en/research/foundation/2019/secure-retirement

Use your mobile device to scan the QR code to go straight to the webpage.

THE PRODUCTIVITY PUZZLE: RESTORING ECONOMIC DYNAMISM

edited by David E. Adler and Laurence B. Siegel

US labor productivity has been stagnating since 2005 onward, averaging growth of only 1.3% a year since then, as opposed to 2.8% annual growth over the previous decade starting in 1995. The United States is not alone: According to McKinsey & Company data, labor productivity growth rates remain near historic lows in many other advanced economies. The slowdown in productivity growth in these economies is a problem—and a puzzle.

The Productivity Puzzle: Restoring Economic Dynamism, edited by David E. Adler and Laurence B. Siegel, is an anthology of essays about this mysterious stagnation in productivity. It provides new policy solutions in addition to analyses of the problem.

The book's central innovation is that it is interdisciplinary. Traditional macroeconomics has trouble fully explaining the productivity puzzle because the sources of productivity growth often lie in a country's specific economic practices and institutions. These institutional differences are better captured by political economists, historians, and social thinkers than by macroeconomists. But productivity also has macroeconomic components, including interest rate regimes and terms and amounts of trade, which are typically missing from political or institutional analyses. That is, neither the macroeconomic nor the institutional approach is adequate to fully capture all the drivers of productivity growth. As a result, the anthology consists of authors writing from multiple perspectives, not just mainstream economics or finance.

The book offers analyses that investors may be unfamiliar with, including statistical debates about productivity measurement and the decline in US manufacturing employment, little-known interest rate mechanisms that might drive misallocations of the economy to lower productivity sectors, and institutional deficiencies in the US innovation "system" that make it hard for those in the United States to translate academic research into actual manufacturing processes as is done in Germany and Japan.

Essays in the anthology explore whether the United States is still a start-up nation, implications for the economy of the rise of superstar firms, and finally, whether the United States is abandoning its commitment to free market competition. The increase in market concentration means that cellphone plans, internet service, and airline tickets are now more expensive in the United States than in Europe.

Contributors to the book come from a variety of backgrounds and tend to have a global perspective. They include central bankers, political scientists who study innovation, financial economists, and the Nobel Laureate Edmund Phelps.

The book consists in part of the proceedings from the landmark conference on productivity and dynamism, organized by the editors, that took place at the Museum of American Finance in New York in November 2017 and of which the CFA Institute Research Foundation was a sponsor, along with other firms and organizations. These proceedings have been augmented here by essays relevant to the topic, selected by the editors.

These new analyses present innovation solutions to the problems the book discusses. Understanding the drivers of productivity stagnation and growth is vitally important for everyone, including investors. As Paul Krugman has said, "Productivity isn't everything, but in the long run, it is almost everything."

We are thus very pleased to present *The Productivity Puzzle: Restoring Economic Dynamism*. We believe it is a substantial contribution to the literature on the sources of, and obstacles to, economic progress.

The publication can be found at

https://www.cfainstitute.org/en/research/foundation/2019/the-productivity-puzzle

Use your mobile device to scan the QR code to go straight to the webpage.

BEHAVIORAL FINANCE: THE SECOND GENERATION

by Meir Statman

Behavioral finance presented in this book is the second generation of behavioral finance. The first generation, starting in the early 1980s, largely accepted standard finance's notion of people's wants as "rational" wants—restricted to the utilitarian benefits of high returns and low risk. That first generation commonly described people as "irrational"—succumbing to cognitive and emotional errors and misled on their way to their rational wants. The second generation describes people as normal. It begins by acknowledging the full range of people's normal wants and their benefits—utilitarian, expressive, and emotional—distinguishes normal wants from errors, and offers guidance on using shortcuts and avoiding errors on the way to satisfying normal wants. People's normal wants include financial security, nurturing children and families, gaining high social status, and staying true to values. People's normal wants, even more than their cognitive and emotional shortcuts and errors, underlie answers to important questions of finance, including saving and spending, portfolio construction, asset pricing, and market efficiency

Second-generation behavioral finance offers an alternative foundation block for each of the five foundation blocks of standard finance, incorporating knowledge about people's wants and their cognitive and emotional shortcuts and errors. According to second-generation behavioral finance,

1. People are normal.

2. People construct portfolios as described by behavioral portfolio theory, where people's portfolio wants extend beyond high expected returns and low risk, such as wants for social responsibility and social status.

3. People save and spend as described by behavioral life-cycle theory, where impediments, such as weak self-control, make it difficult to save and spend in the right way.

4. Expected returns of investments are accounted for by behavioral asset pricing theory, where differences in expected returns are determined by more than just differences in risk—for example, by levels of social responsibility and social status.

5. Markets are not efficient in the sense that price always equals value in them, but they are efficient in the sense that they are hard to beat.

People want three types of benefits—utilitarian, expressive, and emotional—from every activity, product, and service, including financial ones. Utilitarian benefits answer the question, What does something do for me and my wallet? Expressive benefits answer the question, What does something say about me to others and to myself? Emotional benefits answer the question, How does something make me feel?

The book distinguishes cognitive and emotional shortcuts from cognitive and emotional errors. Framing is one cognitive shortcut, such as framing money into two checking accounts, one for the wife and another for the husband, or into a single joint account. Each shortcut involves considerations of utilitarian, expressive, and emotional benefits and costs.

We see framing shortcuts and errors in many financial settings. Official US statistical agencies report monthly or quarterly numbers for GDP, industrial production, inflation, and more. In many other countries, however, statistical agencies report annual numbers.

Reporting data as monthly, quarterly, or annual makes no difference to rational investors because these data are different only in frame, not in substance. Yet financial market prices react more strongly to the most recent number placed in the headline of the press release—the monthly or quarterly number in countries that place that number in the headline and the annual number in countries that place that number in the headline.

Advice to set emotions aside when considering investments and use reason alone is common but wrong for three reasons: First, we cannot set emotions aside even if we want to. Second, emotions are not necessarily emotional errors. Third, emotional shortcuts help more than emotional errors harm. Emotional shortcuts complement reason, and the interaction between emotions and reason is beneficial, often critically so.

A study of financial advertisements showed that compared with neutral imagery, emotionally laden imagery increases investor knowledge about important investment characteristics, such as costs, time to maturity, and dividend frequency. Emotionally laden disclosure of risk factors increases knowledge of risk factors but does not increase knowledge of other investment characteristics. Emotionally laden imagery increases average amounts invested, whereas emotionally laden disclosure of risk decreases the willingness to consider other information.

The efficient market hypothesis is at the center of standard finance, and many believe that behavioral finance refutes it. Indeed, many believe that refutation of the efficient market hypothesis is the most important contribution of behavioral finance. This issue becomes confused, however, when discussants fail to distinguish between two versions of efficient markets and their corresponding efficient market hypotheses—the price-equals-value efficient market hypothesis and the hard-to-beat efficient market hypothesis. And it remains a mystery why so many investors believe that markets are easy to beat.

Both standard finance and behavioral finance provide evidence refuting the value-efficient market hypothesis, but their evidence generally supports the hard-to-beat efficient market hypothesis. Behavioral finance also explains why so many investors believe that markets are easy to beat when, in fact, they are hard to beat.

Value-efficient markets are markets where investment prices always equal their intrinsic values, and the value-efficient market hypothesis is the claim that investment prices always equal their intrinsic values. Hard-to-beat efficient markets are markets wherein some investors are able to beat the market consistently, earning abnormal returns over time, but most are unable to do so. Abnormal returns are returns exceeding the returns one would expect according to a correct asset pricing model.

Value-efficient markets are impossible to beat because abnormal returns come from exploiting discrepancies between prices and values. Such discrepancies are absent in value-efficient markets. But hard-to-beat efficient markets are not necessarily value-efficient markets. It might be that substantial discrepancies between prices and values are common, implying markets far from value efficiency, but discrepancies are hard to identify in time or difficult to exploit for abnormal returns. As I often say, markets are crazy, but this does not make you a psychiatrist.

The publication can be found at

https://www.cfainstitute.org/en/research/foundation/2019/behavioral-finance-the-second-generation

Use your mobile device to scan the QR code to go straight to the webpage.

III. LITERATURE REVIEW SUMMARIES

PERFORMANCE ATTRIBUTION: HISTORY AND PROGRESS

by Carl Bacon, CIPM
summarized by Laurence B. Siegel

Portfolio performance evaluation is a critical aspect of investment management. A proper assessment of performance results can lead to improvements in investment approach, client communications, and portfolio manager incentives, as well as sophisticated, rather than capricious, manager hiring and firing.

Performance evaluation consists of three components: measurement, attribution, and appraisal. Attribution is the attempt to determine which investment decisions over a given period are the source of the active return (positive or negative) of a portfolio relative to its equity. That is, the objective of performance attribution is to explain the source of return of a portfolio, not in isolation, but in relation to a benchmark.

A good attribution system should include a solid theoretical foundation and consistent approach for valuation and analysis. It should also provide the user with the ability to access, analyze, and summarize security details and transactions and convert these inputs into meaningful attribution results. Furthermore, the attribution framework should be consistent with the portfolio's decision-making process and should be compatible with the organization's risk and performance systems.

Performance measurement and evaluation started in the 1960s with efforts to develop methods for comparing the performance of pension funds. Although the analysis was not done relative to a benchmark, the conclusions of the studies conducted in the 1960s are widely accepted today: that market values (not cost) should be used, that total and time-weighted returns are the relevant measure of performance, that risk should be considered as well as return, and that funds should be classified on the basis of their objectives.

The first paper specifically on attribution analysis was written by Eugene Fama in 1972. He provided a decomposition of the sources of observed return into the part related to the ability to select securities at a given level of risk (roughly speaking, alpha) and the part related to general market movements (beta). In the same year, a study by the Society of Investment Analysis in the United Kingdom introduced the ideas of macro (i.e., asset classes or sectors) and micro (i.e., securities within an asset class) levels of decision making and of intermediate notional portfolios to serve as comparators for separating asset allocation and security selection effects.

A series of papers by Gary Brinson and his co-authors in the 1980s separated a portfolio's return in excess of its benchmark into a timing component (i.e., over/underweighting an asset class or sector), a security selection component, and an interaction or cross-product effect (a controversial effect explained in detailed in this literature review). These papers provided the basic formulas for the effects that are commonly used today.

Classical attribution models apply to single-period performance. Although extending this analysis to multiple periods might sound simple, it is not, and as a result, we have no commonly accepted approach to combining attribution effects in a multi-period analysis. Because of compounding, the sum of geometric (compound) return differences does not equal the difference between geometric returns, as is the case with arithmetic returns. Proposed solutions include those that effectively redistribute the residual across the other factors and those that link arithmetic instead of geometric returns. Other authors have proposed exact approaches based on geometric excess returns.

The performance attribution literature has also considered the multicurrency case. One approach extends the Brinson attribution framework to produce a currency return with two components: (1) a forward premium that is predictable because it depends on interest rate differentials and (2) a currency surprise that is uncertain. An influential 1994 paper by Karnosky and Singer resolved the compounding return issue by using continuously compounded returns (which are additive), showed why managing currency separately from markets in a multicurrency portfolio is optimal, and provided an attribution framework for global portfolios.

In practice, the three broad types of attribution approach depend on the information that is needed to calculate the attribution effects: beginning-period positions (holdings-based attribution); beginning-period positions plus purchases and sales (transactions-based attribution), and historical portfolio returns

(returns-based, or factor, attribution). Asset managers will select an approach on the basis of their investment objectives and approaches, data availability, and the cost and complexity of each approach, although a factor attribution can, in general, complement the other two approaches.

The standard allocation/selection model may lead to attribution results that do not reflect the investment process. This issue is an ongoing challenge in the science of performance evaluation. Some authors have proposed using risk-adjusted performance attribution, but it is rarely used in practice.

Classic attribution models focused explicitly or implicitly on equity investments. Fixed-income attribution requires its own model because of the significant differences between the investment decision processes of equity and fixed-income portfolio managers. Typical fixed-income attribution effects include carry (coupon and the rolling-down effect); yield curve (parallel shift, twist, and curvature); spread; selection (convexity and optionality); and other (e.g., currency). No standardized fixed-income attribution approach is available.

In contrast, the standard equity attribution approach can be adapted to derivatives (options, index futures, and swaps) and short positions in general.

Performance attribution has evolved considerably since early work in the 1960s, but current practice continues to rely on the intuition and tools of the classical models. The passage of time has made not only the models but also performance attribution, more broadly, an essential component of the investment management process.

The publication can be found at
https://www.cfainstitute.org/en/research/foundation/2019/performance-attribution

Use your mobile device to scan the QR code to go straight to the webpage.

IV. BRIEFS SUMMARIES

RELATIONSHIP ALPHA: THE EMERGING COMPETITIVE ADVANTAGE IN WEALTH MANAGEMENT

by Charlotte B. Beyer

Book knowledge and behavioral finance expertise can take a firm only so far. Although so-called soft skills are often dismissed as less important than "hard" analytical skills, relationship alpha (α) is a reinvention of the client experience. By balancing the power of EQ (the emotional quotient) with IQ, advisors can use relationship α to enhance every aspect of their client relationships—for the benefit of both the clients and the firm. Earning trust is only the first step; engaging the client (or prospective client) in a genuine dialogue is next and creates true relationship α. Such a dialogue sounds nothing like a skilled analyst drilling down into a company's balance sheet with the CFO. Private clients rarely respond well to such intense examination because their wealth often inspires a fear of being "taken" or fooled, so any dialogue requires skills beyond the tired script of the traditional salesperson.

Within this brief are training exercises for a firm's professionals, the tool of quadrants of sophistication and control for inspiring a dialogue, and five questions to ask clients in order maintain relationship α. Also included are ways to design more successful client reports and create more engaging client meetings.

More controversial in this brief is the author's call for a firm to reexamine several assumptions embraced yesterday but damaging to any firm in today's competitive market. For example, not every senior professional of a firm is suited for the initial marketing to a prospect. Not every CFA charterholder, brand-new or veteran, can learn how to effectively interact with clients. Relationship α requires a continual and rigorous review of the client experience within the context of each firm's unique constraints and resources. Citing examples from the most successful advisors, this brief serves as a step-by-step guide toward transformation of an advisory practice—moving from an archaic business model under attack into a profitable firm inspired by a clear code of conduct, true engagement of all professionals, and highly satisfied clients.

The publication can be found at
https://www.cfainstitute.org/en/research/foundation/2019/beyer-brief

Use your mobile device to scan the QR code to go straight to the webpage.

TEN YEARS AFTER: REFLECTIONS ON THE GLOBAL FINANCIAL CRISIS

by Laurence B. Siegel and Luis Garcia-Feijóo, CFA, CIPM

The *Ten Years After* Brief contains summaries of research articles and central banker discussions from the "2008 Financial Crisis: A Ten-Year Review" conference that took place in November 2018 in New York City. The full versions of the articles were published by the *Annual Review of Financial Economics*, and actual live conference sessions can be accessed via the CFA Institute website.

The summaries in the Brief, which are short descriptions of the original articles, are intended for practitioners and investors interested in learning about the current status of academic research related to the 2008 financial crisis. An edited and annotated transcript of a conversation between central bankers Ben Bernanke, Lord Mervyn King, and Jean-Claude Trichet about the crisis makes the Brief of particular interest.

The 11 articles summarized in the Brief provide an overview of recent research that not only offers insights into the 2008 crisis but also describes lines of inquiry and findings that go beyond understanding the origins of the global financial crisis.

In "Deglobalization: The Rise of Disembedded Unilateralism," Harold James describes the growing opposition to globalization in the wake of the crisis, with an associated decline in cross-border investing and international trade. However, he notes that opposition to globalization may lead to its reform and resurgence.

Gary Gorton relates financial crises to the vulnerability of short-term debt, broadly defined. This vulnerability is inherent in market economies because maturity transformation is an essential function of banks, which in turn are necessary for market economies to exist. Therefore, financial crises have occurred repeatedly throughout history.

Christopher L. Foote and Paul S. Willen review research on mortgage default, which policymakers need to understand better to more effectively respond to financial crises. They note that research supports the view that payment forbearance is an effective way to reduce default. However, defaults by individual borrowers are difficult to predict because they depend on loss-of-income shocks that are unforecastable.

Manuel Adelino, Antoinette Schoar, and Felipe Severino indicate why a proper diagnosis of the reasons for the 2008 financial crisis is necessary to prevent a repeat in the future. They analyze the origins of the crisis and unveil evidence that contradicts some popular beliefs. They conclude that regulators should consider time-varying capital requirements and countercyclical loan-to-value requirements. Matthew Richardson, Kermit L. Schoenholtz, and Lawrence J. White critically discuss the following three levers of recent prudential regulation: capital requirements, liquidity requirements, and regulation of scope. They emphasize that regulators should select the most cost-effective tools to reduce systemic risk. Andrew Metrick and June Rhee provide an overview of reforms that occurred after the financial crisis, organizing their presentation into three types of reforms: preventative, emergency, and restructuring powers. They note that the main effect of the new reforms has been to shift power from emergency into preventative and restricting powers but that some of the new rules are complex and untested.

Deborah Lucas reviews the cost and beneficiaries of the bailouts that took place during the 2008 financial crisis, providing rigor and clarity to the controversy surrounding those bailouts. Tobias Adrian, John Kiff, and Hyun Song Shin review the causes of bank deleveraging following the crisis, making the case that reasons other than increased regulation have been the main cause of deleveraging. Furthermore, they organize post-2008 regulatory reforms around four objectives and conclude that further research is needed on their unintended consequences. Zhiguo He and Arvind Krishnamurthy offer an introduction to the new and growing literature on asset pricing models based on frictions incurred by financial intermediaries.

Robert Engle reviews the impact on financial crises of undercapitalization of financial firms and of the ability of the financial system to withstand the risk created by undercapitalized institutions (risk capacity). He shows evidence that systemic risk has been reduced dramatically since the financial crisis. Stephen G. Ryan reviews recent research connecting financial reporting and financial stability. Specifically, he organizes and reviews the evidence around the following three channels: capital requirement violations, banks' risk management and control systems, and the discipline of markets and regulators over banks.

In the "Central Banker Roundtable," which was moderated by Stanley Fischer, central bankers Ben Bernanke, Lord Mervyn King, and Jean-Claude Trichet provided their views and firsthand accounts of the global financial crisis. The roundtable touched on such topics as the cause and depth of the crisis, the tools available to fight it, the speed of international transmission, and the unprecedented informal coordination among central banks. Other topics covered included the need to regulate maturity transformation and moral hazard and the future of central bank independence.

The topics covered in the roundtable and in the research articles are intertwined and complementary. As a result, the Brief provides an easy-to-read, yet rigorous, assessment of the most relevant research on the global financial crisis, 10 years after it occurred.

The publication can be found at
https://www.cfainstitute.org/en/research/foundation/2019/ten-years-after

Use your mobile device to scan the QR code to go straight to the webpage.

TONTINES: A PRACTITIONER'S GUIDE TO MORTALITY-POOLED INVESTMENTS

by Richard K. Fullmer, CFA

Tontines and similar mortality-pooled investment arrangements offer a useful and unique value proposition to the global retirement challenge.

A tontine is a financial arrangement in which members form an asset pool and agree to receive payouts from it while living and to forfeit their accounts upon death. Forfeited balances are then apportioned among the surviving members. So, members earn not only investment returns but also mortality credits for as long as they survive.

A key feature of tontines is that they pool the longevity risk of their members. Pooling diversifies the risk and allows members the assurance of lifetime income. Because they offer no guarantees, payouts will vary depending on investment performance and the mortality experience of the membership pool. Dispensing with the cost of guarantees allows tontines to be cheaper than comparable insurance products.

The study of tontine design has emerged recently as a specialty of its own. The discipline represents a paradigm shift relative to the disciplines of either traditional investments or insurance. A first step in the study of tontine design is to understand the fair tontine principle.[6] The principle is

---

[6]This principle requires that forfeited balances be transferred to survivors in a manner such that no investor (and, therefore, no class of investor) is unfairly disadvantaged.

quite strict. Yet, as a string enables a strictly bounded kite much freedom to soar, adherence to the fair tontine principle likewise enables the designer a significant (and perhaps surprising) amount of freedom.

Tontines represent an alternative product choice. They might appeal to the following:

- Employers that wish to offer defined benefit–like employee pension plans that can never become underfunded

- Defined contribution plan sponsors that wish to offer participants an option that provides the assurance of annuity-like lifetime income while avoiding the fiduciary liability and counterparty risk associated with selecting an insurance company as guarantor

- Investors who wish to increase their returns without increasing investment risk

- Anyone seeking the assurance of lifetime income with greater transparency and at lower cost than with insurance guarantees

- Policymakers who wish to encourage retiree participation in lifetime income solutions

- Governments that wish to create (or re-create) a market for lifetime income products in countries where annuity markets are nonexistent or dysfunctional

The publication can be found at
https://www.cfainstitute.org/en/research/foundation/2019/tontines

Use your mobile device to scan the QR code to go straight to the webpage.

UNIVERSITY ENDOWMENTS: A PRIMER

by Richard Franz and Stephan Kranner

Endowments have been important for society in their role of supporting good causes over long time horizons. Some of them have a long history of more than five centuries. Today, endowments represent an important class of institutional investors.

This brief focuses on university endowments, which have been at the forefront of exploring new investment styles and asset classes. Some of these endowments have reported outstanding risk-adjusted returns, which allowed them to strongly support their university financially.

On the one hand, these institutions enjoy supportive characteristics that allow them to seek new investment opportunities. First, endowments do not need to fear fund withdrawals. Second, their investment horizon is perpetual, and third, endowments enjoy a special network among their stakeholders. On the other hand, the investment strategy should be consistent with the spending strategy and the fundraising strategy of the endowment. This needs to be continuously monitored within the governance structure of the endowment, which could limit its investment possibilities.

Interestingly, not all university endowments have enjoyed above-market returns. Comparing the average American university endowment with a simple 60% US stock and 40% US bond allocation reveals a similar return and volatility behavior. As with other institutional investors, only a small number of leading institutions are able to exploit the special characteristics university endowments could potentially enjoy. To make use of the full range of investment opportunities, an endowment needs to have access to skilled asset managers and sophisticated investment approaches, which depends on the endowment's size and the network of the institution.

If an endowment has access to such factors, it should be able to generate sustainable, above-market risk-adjusted returns over the long run. If this is not the case, the observation of endowments empirically supports the main advice of financial theory: Diversify and keep asset management costs at a minimum.

The publication can be found at
https://www.cfainstitute.org/en/research/foundation/2019/university-endowments-primer

Use your mobile device to scan the QR code to go straight to the webpage.

A CASH-FLOW FOCUS FOR ENDOWMENTS AND TRUSTS

by James P. Garland, CFA

The primary objective of perpetual endowment funds and long-lived trust funds is to generate spendable cash. Ideally, these cash disbursements would be stable from one year to the next and would grow to keep pace with inflation.

Too-high disbursements today would lead to too-low disbursements tomorrow, and vice versa. Setting a proper spending rate is difficult. Trustees often set percentage spending rates based on the real returns they expect to earn from their investments and then link those spending rates to their funds' market values. But linking spending to market values causes problems.

One problem is that market values of common asset classes, such as stocks and bonds, are volatile. Trustees fight this volatility by averaging market values over time, but averaging does not work very well.

Another problem is that trustees who base spending on market values often understandably come to believe that market values themselves determine spending. In other words, if market values increase (or fall) by a significant amount, then trustees feel justified in increasing (or cutting) spending by similar amounts. This belief is misguided. For equities, the predominant asset class in most endowment and trust funds, the source of returns is not market values but, rather, corporate profits.

This brief argues that, counter to common practice, trustees should turn their backs on market values and instead focus on the real cash flows that their assets can generate. For bonds, this would mean their real interest rate. For equities, this would mean their underlying profits. This focus on asset cash flows, rather than on asset market values, is a better way to go. This brief offers two spending rules based on cash flows. One looks at corporate dividends, and the other at corporate profits.

Trustees who base spending on market values usually include bonds in their funds to dampen market value swings. A 30% bond allocation is not uncommon. Yet the cash-flow spending rules described here lead to less volatile spending, even when applied to a 100% equity portfolio, than that of a 30% bond/70% equity portfolio whose spending is based on market values.

In addition, spending rules based on cash flows free trustees from fretting about market values. Diversification can still be beneficial, but no longer do trustees need to diversify primarily to dampen market downturns. When equity market values decline, as they invariably will from time to time, trustees may be able to say, "We don't care."

Furthermore, spending rules based on cash flows enable trustees to keep score. Trustees of perpetual endowment funds and of long-lived personal trust funds often feel obligated to be intergenerationally equitable—that is, to treat current and future beneficiaries the same. The near-universal way to evaluate intergenerational equity is to look at market values. Instead, a spending rule based on cash flows works better.

Finally, basing spending on cash flows, rather than on market values, encourages trustees to focus on something that is very important but often overlooked: the long-term health of the economies in which their funds are invested.

No spending rule is perfect. But many trustees who now base spending on market values would benefit by focusing on asset cash flows instead.

The publication can be found at

https://www.cfainstitute.org/en/research/foundation/2019/cash-flow-focus-endowments-trusts

Use your mobile device to scan the QR code to go straight to the webpage.

AFRICAN CAPITAL MARKETS: CHALLENGES AND OPPORTUNITIES

edited by Heidi Raubenheimer, CFA

Every piece in this CFA Institute Research Foundation brief tells of a market in Africa: where it's going and where it's coming from. In conjunction with the African Securities Exchanges Association (ASEA) and CFA Institute local societies, authors from South Africa, Nigeria, Mauritius, Ghana, Zimbabwe, Morocco, Egypt, Botswana, and the East African community have all contributed to the brief, providing authoritative insights and analysis for current and prospective investors in African capital markets.

The brief highlights the critical role of stock exchanges in the global economy: Exchange businesses contribute to the economic objectives of their jurisdictions—raising money and investing—but they also have a social responsibility to prudently allocate resources and create employment, among other obligations.

Some of the exchanges you'll read about in the brief were established in early colonial times. South Africa led the way on the heels of the diamond and gold rush, followed by Zimbabwe, Egypt, and Namibia—all before 1905. Some of these didn't outlive the commodities rush, but others are still thriving today, substantially diversified and modernised from their beginnings over a century ago. Some capital markets on the continent were established more recently, and their development tells of independence and nation building: Nigeria in the 1960s; Botswana, Mauritius, and Ghana in 1989; Namibia (post-independence from South Africa) in the 1990s. Still others—particularly the East African exchanges—are brand new and leapfrogging toward greater participation. All of these tell of how regulation, trading technology, and fintech are enabling fairer, faster, and lower-cost participation in finance and investment for more market participants.

Africa is now home to 36 stock exchanges serving 43 economies and representing 1,400 listed companies with a turnover of USD41.14 billion. These markets have grown steadily and demonstrated their capability to create prosperity on the continent.

The publication can be found at
https://www.cfainstitute.org/en/research/foundation/2019/african-capital-markets

Use your mobile device to scan the QR code to go straight to the webpage.

V. WORKSHOP FOR THE PRACTITIONER SUMMARIES

THE FUTURE OF INVESTMENT MANAGEMENT

by Ronald N. Kahn

This presentation for the 2019 CFA Institute Research Foundation Workshop for the Practitioner addressed issues covered in my book *The Future of Investment Management*.

Investment management is in flux, arguably more than it has been in a long time. Active management is under pressure, with investors switching from active to index funds. New "smart beta" products offer low-cost exposures to many active ideas. Exchange-traded funds are proliferating. Markets and regulations have changed significantly over the past 10–20 years, and data and technology—which are increasingly important for investment management—are evolving even more rapidly.

In the midst of this change, what can we say about the future of investment management? What ideas will influence its evolution? What types of products will flourish over the next 5–10 years?

I use a long perspective to address these questions. I analyze the modern intellectual history of investment management—roughly, the set of ideas, developed over the past 100 years, that have influenced investment management up to now. For additional context and to understand the full arc of history, I briefly discuss the early roots of the field. As I discuss this history, I review the various ideas and insights that ultimately coalesce into a coherent understanding of investing, in spite of its uncertain nature.

One central theme that emerges is that investment management is becoming increasingly systematic. Over time, our understanding of risk has evolved from a general aversion to losing money to a precisely defined statistic we can measure and forecast. Our understanding of expected returns has evolved as the necessary data have become more available, as our understanding of fundamental value has developed, and as we have slowly come to understand the connection between return and risk and the relevance of human behavior to both. Data and technology have advanced in parallel to facilitate implementing better approaches.

Our systems of understanding this intrinsically uncertain activity of investing continue to expand, affecting the investment products we see today and those we expect to see in the future. It is as hard to imagine index funds and exchange-traded funds dominating the investment markets of the Netherlands in the 1700s as it is to imagine their absence in the global investment markets of 2018.

With an understanding of the ideas underlying investment management today, including several insights into active management, I discuss the many trends currently roiling the field. These trends, applied to the current state of investment management, suggest that investment management will evolve into three distinct branches—indexing, smart beta/factor investing, and pure alpha investing, where "pure alpha" refers to active returns above and beyond those arising from static exposures to smart beta factors. Each branch will offer two styles of products: those that focus exclusively on returns and those that include goals beyond returns.

The following is a chapter-by-chapter summary of the book. Chapter 1 provides an overview and introduction. Chapter 2, on the early roots of investment management, briefly defines investment management and discusses its development. What is investment management, what are its required elements, and when did those elements first appear? Investment management may go back to ancient times, but its clear historical record begins in the Netherlands in the late 1700s. Those early records show that investors already appreciated diversification and thought about value investing.

Chapter 3, on the modern history of investment management, traces the evolution of ideas and practices that have influenced the field up through today. The first efforts at developing systematic approaches began almost a century ago, partly in response to periods of wild speculation and losses like the market crash of 1929. Our understanding of investment value developed around this time, and our modern understanding of risk and portfolio construction began in the 1950s. Chapter 3 also traces the development of ideas underlying index funds—initially conceived in academia in the 1960s—and, in response, the eventual development of systematic approaches to active management.

Chapter 4, on seven insights into active management, describes key concepts required to understand efforts to outperform. This chapter begins with the "arithmetic of active management," the idea that active management is worse than a zero-sum game—that the average active manager will underperform. It then shows that the information ratio—the amount of outperformance per unit of risk—determines an active manager's ability to add value for investors. It also determines how investors should allocate risk and capital to different active products. The chapter discusses the fundamental law of active management, which breaks down the information ratio into constituent parts: skill, diversification, and efficiency. This relationship can help active managers develop new strategies and provide some guidance to investors looking to choose active managers. Other insights cover the process of forecasting returns, challenges to testing new investment ideas, and understanding how portfolio constraints affect the efficiency of implementing investment ideas.

Chapter 5, on seven trends in investment management, turns the spotlight on current directions that will influence the future of the field. These trajectories include the shift in assets from active to passive investing, the increase in competition among active managers, the changing market environment, the emergence of big data, the development of smart beta, the increased interest in what I call investing beyond returns—that is, investing for non-return objectives, such as environmental, social, and governance goals, as well as to earn returns—and, finally, fee compression.

Chapter 6, on the future of investment management, applies these trends to the current state of investment management—theory and practice—to forecast how the field will evolve over the next 5–10 years. As noted previously, I expect investment management to evolve into three distinct branches, with each offering two styles of products.

The investment case for indexing is compelling. Successful indexing is all about delivering exposures as cheaply and reliably as possible. The ability to provide exposures cheaply requires scale, and indexing is already dominated by a few very large firms. Although things could always go wrong in investment management, nothing would systemically threaten indexing as an investment category.

The investment case for smart beta/factor investing is fairly strong, if not as strong as the case for indexing. Like indexing, these products attempt to deliver exposures as cheaply as possible. I expect consolidation over time. A small number of firms will manage most of the smart beta/factor assets. Several things could threaten this branch of investment management: poor performance over an extended period, severe poor performance over a short period due to large and correlated outflows, and a lack of investor understanding of expected dispersion across different smart beta/factor funds.

Pure alpha investing faces the most difficult investment case—I expect the average pure alpha investor to underperform—though there are reasons to believe that some pure alpha investors can succeed. Pure alpha investing is distinctly not about delivering exposure cheaply. Instead, it involves narrow and transient ideas that require constant innovation to replace old ideas the market comes to understand. Pure alpha is capacity constrained and expensive. The most successful pure alpha firms will be research-driven boutiques, possibly including boutiques within large asset management firms. Although plenty can go wrong with individual pure alpha products, I do not see systemic threats to this branch of investing.

To add an optimistic spin on the current level of disruption in investment management, which is unsettling for many people in the field, I believe that disruption can create great opportunities. The shifting boundaries between active and passive and dramatic changes in technology augur well for new types of products and new sources of information to help managers outperform. Today may not be a great time to be a 50-year-old investment manager, but as I often tell students and colleagues studying for the CFA® Program exams, it is a great time to be a quantitatively oriented 28-year-old entering the field.

To view the video, visit:

https://www.cfainstitute.org/en/research/multimedia/2019/future-of-investment-management

The publication can be found at:

https://www.cfainstitute.org/en/research/foundation/2018/future-of-investment-management

POPULARITY: A BRIDGE BETWEEN CLASSICAL AND BEHAVIORAL FINANCE

by Roger G. Ibbotson, Thomas M. Idzorek, CFA, Paul D. Kaplan, CFA, and James X. Xiong, CFA

This presentation for the 2019 CFA Institute Research Foundation Workshop for the Practitioner addressed issues covered in our book *Popularity: A Bridge between Classical and Behavioral Finance*.

Popularity is a word that embraces how much anything is liked, recognized, or desired. Popularity drives demand. In this book, we apply this concept to assets and securities to explain the premiums and so-called anomalies in security markets, especially the stock market.

Most assets and securities have a relatively fixed supply over the short or intermediate term. Popularity represents the demand for a security—or perhaps the set of reasons why a security is demanded to the extent that it is—and thus is an important determinant of prices for a given set of expected cash flows.

A common belief in the finance literature is that premiums in the market are payoffs for the *risk* of securities—that is, they are "risk" premiums. In classical finance, investors are risk averse, and market frictions are usually assumed away. In the broadest context, risk is unpopular. The largest risk premium is the equity risk premium (i.e., the extra expected return for investing in equities rather than bonds or risk-free assets). Other risk premiums include, for example, the interest rate term premium (because of the greater risk of longer-term bonds) and the default risk premium in bond markets.

There are many premiums in the market that may or may not be related to risk, but all are related to investing in something that is unpopular in some way. We consider premiums to be the result of characteristics that are systematically *unpopular*—that is, popularity makes the price of a security higher and the expected return lower, all other things being equal. Preferences that influence relative popularity can and do change over time. These premiums include the size premium, the value premium, the liquidity premium, the severe downside premium, low volatility and low beta premiums, ESG premiums and discounts, competitive advantage, brand, and reputation. In general, any type of security with characteristics that tend to be overlooked or unwanted can have a premium.

The title of this book refers to a bridge between classical and behavioral finance. Both approaches to finance rest on investor preferences, which we cast as popularity.

In classical finance, risk (and in particular, systematic risk) is the primary asset characteristic to which investors are averse. The CAPM says that all assets are priced according to a single, systematic factor—namely, "market risk" or covariance with the capitalization-weighted market portfolio. In contrast, we believe that risks can also be multi-dimensional, including various types of stock or bond risks. The specific structure of risk and different types of risk can also be priced, such as catastrophic risk. Although classical finance usually assumes away market frictions, rational investors may have preferences for market liquidity, favorable tax treatments, or asset divisibility, making assets more or less valuable to the extent they embody these characteristics.

In behavioral finance, investors may not be completely rational. Thus, investors may have preferences that go beyond rational behavior. We classify behavioral biases into two distinct types, psychological and cognitive. Psychological desires cause some assets to be more popular than others, relative to their expected cash flow and relative to other rational characteristics, such as liquidity. Investors' rationality is also limited because they make cognitive errors.

Neoclassical economics provides the rationality framework for efficient capital markets. Behavioral economics assumes limited or "bounded" rationality and thus provides the framework for prospect theory, loss aversion, framing, mental accounting, overconfidence, and other inconsistencies with rational behavior. Popularity represents all of our preferences, which can be rational or irrational, providing a bridge between classical and behavioral finance.

The CAPM is an elegant and easy-to-use theory for describing investor expected returns in an equilibrium setting. It assumes that investors are rational and risk averse. Because they can diversify away from all non-market risk, only systematic market risk in securities is priced. Securities with higher systematic risk have lower relative prices and thus higher expected returns. We introduce a new formal asset pricing model, the popularity asset pricing model (PAPM), that extends the CAPM to include all types of preferences.

The PAPM is an outgrowth of New Equilibrium Theory (NET), a framework proposed by Ibbotson, Diermeier, and Siegel (*Financial Analysts Journal*, 1984) in which investors are rational but have preferences for or aversions to various security characteristics beyond the single market risk of the CAPM. Additionally, NET goes beyond the multiple dimensions of risk that might be modeled in the arbitrage pricing theory (APT). In NET, in addition to systematic risk aversion, investors have a rational aversion to assets that are difficult to diversify, are less liquid, are highly taxed, or are not easily divisible. All of these preferences impact the prices and expected returns of assets that embody these characteristics.

The PAPM goes even further, providing a theory in an equilibrium framework by including both risk aversion and popularity preferences on the part of the investors. These preferences can be rational, as in NET, or irrational, as in behavioral economics. In the PAPM, securities have a variety of characteristics or dimensions of popularity:

different systematic or unsystematic risks and a variety of additional attributes that some or all investors care about. All of these characteristics are priced according to the aggregate demand for each of the characteristics. The expected return of each security is determined by its risk and other popularity characteristics.

The concept of a *negative return to popularity* (which we shorten to just "popularity") has been shown to be consistent with the empirical premiums found in the stock market. But it is an explanation after the fact. More direct tests involve identifying in advance what characteristics are likely to be popular and then comparing the performance of stocks that should be unpopular with that of stocks that should be popular based on those characteristics.

We did this for five characteristics. First, we argue that companies with high brand values are popular. These companies end up having significantly lower returns than those with the lowest brand value over our period of study. Second, we argue that companies with wide economic moats, having a sustainable competitive advantage, are more popular. We found that companies with no moat outperform the wide moat companies. Third, we found that companies with a better reputation tend to underperform companies with a worse one. Fourth, we argue that stocks that have had historical negative tail risk events (low or negative coskewness) are unpopular. We found that these stocks significantly outperformed those with high coskewness over the period of study. Finally, we argue that stocks with positive historical skewness are popular because they provide the apparent opportunity for outsized gains. We found that these stocks have the lowest risk-adjusted returns over our period of study.

When we did our five direct tests of the popularity hypothesis, we looked at both equally weighted composites and market capitalization-weighted composites of the stocks, giving us 10 tests. While all results, to a moderate or high degree, were consistent with the popularity hypothesis, only 5 out of 10 were consistent with the "more risk equals more return" paradigm.

We also tested most of the well-known premiums and anomalies for consistency with popularity. We found that low-beta, low-volatility, small-cap, value, and less liquid stocks, being less popular, outperformed their more popular counterparts. To do this, we looked at 10 of the factor tests in Ibbotson and Kim (working paper, 2017) through the popularity lens. Of the 10 different factors that we looked at, we found that 7 were consistent with the popularity hypothesis while only 2 were consistent with the "more risk equals more return" paradigm. We also found that within the stock market, the portfolios formed based on these characteristics had an inverse relationship between risk and return, counter to classical theory. Either risk is popular under some circumstances, or other non-risk characteristics dominate returns. We believe that popularity reflects the demand that ultimately determines prices and returns.

The numerous empirical flaws of the CAPM, and the notion that more risk should equate to more return, have given rise to a variety of behavioral based explanations for observed asset prices. Popularity in general, and the PAPM in particular, unifies the driving factors that impact price in the classical finance CAPM world with those that drive price in a behavioral asset pricing world. In this way, popularity creates a unifying theory—a bridge between classical and behavioral finance.

To view the video, visit:

https://www.cfainstitute.org/en/research/multimedia/2019/popularity-a-bridge-between-classical-and-behavioral-finance

The publication can be found at:

https://www.cfainstitute.org/en/research/foundation/2018/popularity-bridge-between-classical-and-behavioral-finance

VI. AWARDS AND RECOGNITION

JAMES R. VERTIN AWARD

The James R. Vertin Award is presented periodically to recognize individuals who have produced a body of research notable for its relevance and enduring value to investment professionals. This award was established in 1996 to honor James R. Vertin, CFA, for his outstanding leadership in promoting excellence and relevancy in research and education.

2019 Vertin Award Winner

John C. Bogle

John C. Bogle may have been one of the very few people who transformed the quest for average into a multi-trillion-dollar industry. To be fair, it was no ordinary quest for average. The goal was not only to earn the market average but also to do so with very low fees so that the average (non-professional) investor could benefit. Bogle's solution was also far from ordinary: founding The Vanguard Group and propelling index mutual funds (and indexing in general) to stardom.

When Bogle founded Vanguard in 1974, mutual funds admittedly had been in existence for years—by some accounts since 1822 in the Netherlands. As for the genesis of index funds, it may go back to an article by Edward Renshaw and Paul Feldstein, "The Case for an Unmanaged Investment Company," published in the January/February 1960 issue of the *Financial Analysts Journal*.

But in 1976, the concepts of mutual funds and index funds came together with Bogle's creation of the Vanguard 500 Index Fund. Originally derided as "Bogle's folly," the Vanguard 500 Index Fund took a while to catch on; yet the introduction of an indexed mutual fund marked a sea change in the financial industry—for investors and investment managers alike. Nobel Prize–winning economist Paul Samuelson saw it as the opposite of foolish. As he said in a speech to the Boston Society of Security Analysts on 15 November 2005, "I rank this Bogle invention along with the invention of the wheel, the alphabet, Gutenberg printing, and wine and cheese."

Like many inventions, Bogle's did not spring up overnight. The seed was planted in 1949 when he was trying to find a topic for his senior thesis at Princeton University and read an article from *Fortune* magazine (December 1949), "Big Money in Boston." The article discussed something Bogle had never encountered: mutual funds. Determined to conduct original research, Bogle was pleased that the industry was characterized as "pretty small change, . . . rapidly expanding and somewhat contentious, . . . the ideal champion of the small stockholder in controversies with . . . corporate management."

Articulated in 1951 in his thesis, "The Economic Role of the Investment Company," are principles remarkably predictive of the approach Bogle favored during his 60-odd years in the investment profession. Ever straightforward, Bogle asserted that mutual funds should be managed efficiently, honestly, and economically; fees and charges should be as low as possible; and the primary responsibility should always be to shareowners, not managers. Moreover, almost predicting indexing—Vanguard's signature approach—Bogle declared that "funds can make no claim to superiority over the market averages."

Hired after college by Wellington Management's founder, Walter L. Morgan, who became his beloved mentor, Bogle spent his entire career in the mutual fund industry, eventually transforming it. At Wellington's headquarters in Philadelphia, Bogle worked alongside A. Moyer Kulp, CFA, and Edmund A. Mennis, CFA, early leaders of what we now know as CFA Institute.

Bogle's idealism was never more evident than in his creation of Vanguard. Founded on the inviolable principle of fiduciary responsibility to shareowners that he articulated in his thesis back in 1951, it was—and is—a truly mutual fund company, owned by those who invest in it. In addition, the phrase "costs matter" is one that was frequently spoken by Bogle. So, it should come as no surprise that Bogle blended those two guiding principles when creating Vanguard.

Bogle was thought of as "Saint Jack" by countless shareowners to whom he delivered their fair share. Yet, as one who frequently and forthrightly criticized the financial industry and consistently advocated for low fees, he also had his detractors. "Bogle has not won any popularity contests among his professional colleagues," noted former Federal Reserve chairman Paul Volcker in his foreword to *John Bogle on Investing: The First 50 Years*. In 1976, the chairman of Fidelity Investments, Edward C. Johnson III, told the Boston Globe that "I can't believe that the great mass of investors are going to be satisfied with an ultimate goal of just achieving average returns on their funds." By 1990, Johnson must have become a believer because Fidelity Investments added its first (and certainly not its last) index fund.

Many in finance, however, have deeply appreciated Bogle's positive effect. In his 2016 Letter to Shareholders, Warren Buffett declared, "If a statue is ever erected to honor the person who has done the most for American investors, the hands-down choice should be Jack Bogle." And Katrina Sherrerd, CFA, former managing director at CFA Institute and someone who worked with Bogle over the years, put it well when she said:

> There is only one Jack! I have never met anyone with as much

conviction, clarity, and commitment to their views and ideals. When Jack sets his mind to doing something, neither doubt nor obstacle will derail him from his desired course. Investors should be grateful that he was committed to being an investor advocate for so many years.

One theme that was consistent throughout Bogle's life was his commitment to education and professionalism. He wrote 10 books and countless articles (including 16 for CFA Institute) and was a frequent speaker advocating for an industry where shareowners (not managers) come first, for low-fee investment vehicles, and for the professionalism of investment management. As he said in a speech at the CFA Institute Annual Conference in 2017:

Strong ethics and professional competence must still be the bulwark of finance. We must develop a keener awareness of how our financial system works, a profound introspection about how we can make it better, a knowledge of the long history of finance, and a deep involvement in fostering in our profession the high character it requires.

By any measure of success, Bogle was successful. But all of his success, perhaps ironically, was achieved by simply targeting the average—capturing the market average and doing so in a way that benefits the average investor. In the hands of John Bogle, average never looked so good.

RESEARCH FOUNDATION LEADERSHIP CIRCLE

The Research Foundation Leadership Circle honors investment professionals whose outstanding commitment and contributions have benefited the Research Foundation over an extended period of time. The Research Foundation is honored to recognize the following members of the Leadership Circle:

Gary P. Brinson, CFA

George Noyes, CFA

Walter Stern, CFA

Fred H. Speece, Jr., CFA

Frank K. Reilly, CFA

© 2020 CFA Institute Research Foundation. All rights reserved.

VII. RECENT PUBLICATIONS

RECENT PUBLICATIONS FROM THE RESEARCH FOUNDATION ARCHIVE

2018

Monographs

Alternative Investments: A Primer for Investment Trustees (March)

Donald R. Chambers, CAIA, Keith Black, CFA, CAIA, and Nelson J. Lacey

Alternative Investments: A Primer for Investment Professionals provides an overview of alternative investments for institutional asset allocators and other overseers of portfolios containing both traditional and alternative assets. It is designed for those with substantial experience regarding traditional investments in stocks and bonds but limited familiarity regarding alternative assets, alternative strategies, and alternative portfolio management.

The primer categorizes alternative assets into four groups: hedge funds, real assets, private equity, and structured products/derivatives. Real assets include vacant land, farmland, timber, infrastructure, intellectual property, commodities, and private real estate. For each group, the primer provides essential information about the characteristics, challenges, and purposes of these institutional-quality alternative assets in the context of a well-diversified institutional portfolio.

Other topics addressed by this primer include tail risk, due diligence of the investment process and operations, measurement and management of risks and returns, setting return expectations, and portfolio construction. The primer concludes with a chapter on the case for investing in alternatives.

https://www.cfainstitute.org/en/research/foundation/2018/alternative-investments-a-primer-for-investment-professionals

The Future of Investment Management (November)

Ronald N. Kahn

Investment management is in flux, arguably more than it has been in a long time. Active management is under pressure, with investors switching from active to index funds. New "smart beta" products offer low-cost exposures to many active ideas. Exchange-traded funds are proliferating. Markets and regulations have changed significantly over the past 10–20 years, and data and technology—which are increasingly important for investment management—are evolving even more rapidly.

In the midst of this change, what can we say about the future of investment management? What ideas will influence its evolution? What types of products will flourish over the next 5–10 years?

I use a long perspective to address these questions and analyze the modern intellectual history of investment management—the set of ideas that have influenced investment management up to now.

https://www.cfainstitute.org/en/research/foundation/2018/future-of-investment-management

Popularity: A Bridge between Classical and Behavioral Finance (December)

Roger G. Ibbotson, Thomas M. Idzorek, CFA, Paul D. Kaplan, CFA, and James X. Xiong, CFA

Popularity is a word that embraces how much anything is liked, recognized, or desired. Popularity drives demand. In this book, we apply this concept to assets and securities to explain the premiums and so-called anomalies in security markets, especially the stock market.

The title of this book refers to a bridge between classical and behavioral finance. Both approaches to finance rest on investor preferences, which we cast as popularity.

https://www.cfainstitute.org/en/research/foundation/2018/popularity-bridge-between-classical-and-behavioral-finance

Literature Reviews

"The Current State of Quantitative Equity Investing" (June)

Ying L. Becker and Marc R. Reinganum

Quantitative equity management is concerned with rigorous, disciplined approaches to help investors structure optimal portfolios to achieve the outcomes they seek. At the root of disciplined, modern investment processes are two things: risk and return. The notion of total return is obvious—price appreciation plus any dividend payments. Risk may not be so straightforward. In most quantitative approaches, risk is viewed as more akin to a roulette wheel; that is, the possible outcomes are well specified and the likelihood of each outcome is known, but in advance, an investor does not know which outcome will be realized.

In this piece, we curate the history of quantitative equity investing, which traces its origins to the development of portfolio theory and the capital asset pricing model (CAPM). In equities, some of the first quantitative approaches were aimed at confirming the theoretical predictions of the CAPM. In particular, the expected return of a risky asset depends only on the risk of that asset as measured by its beta, a covariance measure of risk. In this paradigm, all investors hold the same risky portfolio, the market portfolio of risky assets that maximizes the Sharpe ratio. At the same time, stock prices are viewed to be informationally efficient and reflecting all available information.

https://www.cfainstitute.org/en/research/foundation/2018/current-state-of-quantitative-equity-investing

Briefs

Foundations of High-Yield Analysis (August)

edited by Martin S. Fridson, CFA

This Research Foundation brief explores various dimensions of the high-yield bond market. One contributor decomposes returns and relates risk and associated risk premiums via an econometric fair value model. Another illustrates principles of credit analysis via a case study involving a debt-financed merger. A third analytical piece focuses on forecasting the default rate. Two remaining contributions are primers—one on the corporate bankruptcy process and the other on high-yield bond covenants. The final section presents high-yield price histories as a function of macroeconomic forces, impulse forces, risk, and technical features of the time series themselves.

https://www.cfainstitute.org/en/research/foundation/2018/foundations-of-high-yield-analysis

Latin American Local Capital Markets: Challenges and Solutions (June)

edited by Mauro Miranda, CFA

Economic growth depends on the efficient allocation of resources, including the two main factors of production: labor and capital. Markets, operating on each factor, have allocated these resources in economies worldwide in ways that arguably approach optimality and have fostered economic development for the benefit of billions. Capital markets, both for debt and equity securities, have allowed firms to secure funding for productive uses while providing investors with opportunities for portfolio diversification. The importance of capital markets for the development of economies and for the betterment of society cannot be overstated.

This is just as true in emerging economies with free markets, such as those found in Latin America, as it is in developed markets. However, capital markets in the region are not being utilized to the fullest. What challenges face Latin American countries in the development of their local capital markets? How can these countries unlock the true potential of their markets and thus spur growth?

The idea behind this collection of articles is to offer a primer on the development of local capital markets in several select countries in Latin America. We discuss not only their history and current status but also their future. To this end, seven authors contributed to this project, each writing about one of seven countries: Argentina, Brazil, Chile, Colombia, Mexico, Peru, and Uruguay. Each author decided which issues they believe matter most to the progress of their local capital markets. Some authors chose a qualitative and institutional description of local markets, whereas others adopted a more quantitative approach.

https://www.cfainstitute.org/en/research/foundation/2018/latin-american-local-capital-markets

Mainstreaming Sustainable Investing (October)

edited by Michael J. Greis, CFA

"Mainstreaming Sustainable Investing" is the title, tagline, and guiding principle of the annual Sustainable Investing Seminars run by CFA Society Boston since 2013. In that first year, the idea of "mainstreaming" sustainable investing seemed wildly aspirational to many. Yet by the time the society held its fourth annual seminar in November 2016, aspiration had been surpassed by reality, as the increasing attendance and diversity of the audience reflected the change that was underway in the industry.

https://www.cfainstitute.org/en/research/foundation/2018/mainstreaming-sustainable-investing

Risk Tolerance and Circumstances (March)

Elke U. Weber and Joachim Klement, CFA

An investor's risk attitude is a stable characteristic, like a personality trait, but risk-taking behavior can change based on the investor's age, recent market events, and life experiences. These factors change investors' perceptions of the risks. Differences in risk tolerance between men and women or in different circumstances trace back to emotional as much as rational considerations. Financial advisers should consider all of these factors when advising clients and can use four simple steps to incorporate best practices: be aware, educate, nudge, and hand hold.

https://www.cfainstitute.org/en/research/foundation/2018/risk-tolerance-and-circumstances

Risk Profiling and Tolerance: Insights for the Private Wealth Manager (June)

edited by Joachim Klement, CFA

If risk aversion and willingness to take on risk are driven by emotions and we as humans are bad at correctly identifying them, the finance profession has a serious challenge at hand—how to reliably identify the individual risk profile of a retail investor or high-net-worth individual. In this series of CFA Institute Research Foundation briefs, we have asked academics and practitioners to summarize the current state of knowledge about risk profiling in different key areas.

https://www.cfainstitute.org/en/research/foundation/2018/risk-profiling-and-tolerance

Some Like It Hedged (November)

Momtchil Pojarliev

Foreign currency exposure is a by-product of international investing. When obtaining global asset exposure, investors also obtain the embedded foreign currency exposure. Left unmanaged, this currency exposure acts like a buy-and-hold currency strategy, which receives little or no risk premium and adds unwanted volatility. In "Some Like It Hedged," the author shows that the impact of foreign currency exposure on institutional portfolios depends significantly on the base currency of the investors and the specific composition of their portfolios. In general, investors whose base currency is negatively correlated with global equities, as are the US dollar and the Japanese yen, will reduce the volatility of their portfolios by fully hedging foreign currency exposure. In contrast, investors whose home currency is positively correlated with global equities, as is the Canadian dollar, will benefit from keeping some unhedged foreign currency exposure—in particular, exposure to the US dollar. Finally, investors with larger allocations to domestic assets will experience only small reductions in volatility from hedging.

https://www.cfainstitute.org/en/research/foundation/2018/some-like-it-hedged

2017

Monographs

Equity Valuation: Science, Art, or Craft? (December)

Frank J. Fabozzi, CFA, Sergio M. Focardi, and Caroline Jonas

The price at which a stock is traded in the market reflects the ability of the firm to generate cash flow and the risks associated with generating the expected future cash flows. The authors point to the limits of widely used valuation techniques. The most important of these limits is the inability to forecast cash flows and to determine the appropriate discount rate. Another important limit is the inability to determine absolute value. Widely used valuation techniques such as market multiples—the price-to-earnings ratio, firm value multiples, or a use of multiple ratios, for example—capture only relative value, that is, the value of a firm's stocks related to the value of comparable firms (assuming that comparable firms can be identified).

The study underlines additional problems when it comes to valuing IPOs and private equity: Both are sensitive to the timing of the offer, suffer from information asymmetry, and are more subject to behavioral elements than is the case for shares of listed firms. In the case of IPOs in particular, the authors discuss how communication strategies and media hype play an important role in the IPO valuation/pricing process.

https://www.cfainstitute.org/en/research/foundation/2017/equity-valuation-science-art-or-craft

Handbook on Sustainable Investments: Background Information and Practical Examples for Institutional Asset Owners (December)

Swiss Sustainable Finance

A fast growing share of investors have recently widened their scope of analysis to criteria regarded as extra-financial. They are driven by different motivations. Adoption of sustainable investment strategies can be driven, on the one hand, by the sole motivation to hedge portfolios against knowable risks by expanding the conceptual framework to incorporate the latest best practice in risk management. Other investors focus rather on a long-term view and make an active bet on societal change. Recent empirical research has shown that considering sustainability factors within investment practices does not come at a cost (i.e., through a reduced opportunity set) but allows for competitive returns. Furthermore, the growing market and resulting competition in the wake of sustainable investing going mainstream has the welcome effect to compress fees for such products. Hence, staying informed about recent trends in sustainable investing is imperative no matter what the main motivation is.

https://www.cfainstitute.org/en/research/foundation/2017/handbook-on-sustainable-investments

A Primer for Investment Trustees: Understanding Investment Committee Responsibilities (October)

Jeffery V. Bailey, CFA, and Thomas M. Richards, CFA

This "primer," written as if addressed to a new investment trustee for a university, is a comprehensive discussion of investment issues relevant not only to investment trustees but also to investment professionals who work with trustees. Taking an individual step by step through the process of responsible trusteeship, it offers a solid introduction to basic investment principles.

https://www.cfainstitute.org/en/research/foundation/2017/a-primer-for-investment-trustees

Literature Reviews

"The Equity Risk Premium: A Contextual Literature Review" (November)

Laurence B. Siegel

Research into the equity risk premium, often considered the most important number in finance, falls into three broad groupings. First, researchers have measured the margin by which equity total returns have exceeded fixed-income or cash returns over long historical periods and have projected this measure of the equity risk premium into the future. Second, the dividend discount model—or a variant of it, such as an earnings discount model—is used to estimate the future return on an equity index, and the fixed-income or cash yield is then subtracted to arrive at an equity risk premium expectation or forecast. Third, academics have used macroeconomic techniques to estimate what premium investors might rationally require for taking the risk of equities. Current thinking emphasizes the second, or dividend discount, approach and projects an equity risk premium centered on 3½% to 4%.

https://www.cfainstitute.org/en/research/foundation/2017/equity-risk-premium

Briefs

New Vistas in Risk Profiling (August)

Greg B. Davies

Risk profiling is fraught with misunderstandings that lead to ill-advised approaches to determining suitable investment solutions for individuals. The author discusses how we should think about the crucial elements of (a) risk tolerance, (b) behavioural risk attitudes, and (c) risk capacity. He uses a simple thought experiment to examine a stripped-down investor situation and define the essential features and exact role of each of the components of an investor's overall risk profile. He examines options for eliciting and measuring risk tolerance and considers some promising avenues for future methods.

https://www.cfainstitute.org/en/research/foundation/2017/new-vistas-in-risk-profiling

Asian Structured Products (August)

Angel Wu and Clarke Pitts

In this brief, we examine the nature of structured products, why they are used, and by whom. We consider the size of the industry and some of its most popular products in the context of Asian capital markets. Finally, we identify a variety of risks for each of the parties involved: issuers, intermediaries, and investors.

https://www.cfainstitute.org/en/research/foundation/2017/asian-structured-products

FinTech and RegTech in a Nutshell, and the Future in a Sandbox (July)

Douglas W. Arner, Jànos Barberis, and Ross P. Buckley

The 2008 global financial crisis represented a pivotal moment that separated prior phases of the development of financial technology (FinTech) and regulatory technology (RegTech) from the current paradigm. Today, FinTech has entered a phase of rapid development marked by the proliferation of startups and other new entrants, such as IT and ecommerce firms that have fragmented the financial services market. This new era presents fresh challenges for regulators and highlights why the evolution of FinTech necessitates a parallel development of RegTech. In particular, regulators must develop a robust new framework that promotes innovation and market confidence, aided by the use of regulatory "sandboxes." Certain RegTech developments today are highlighting the path toward another paradigm shift, which will be marked by a reconceptualization of the nature of financial regulation.

https://www.cfainstitute.org/en/research/foundation/2017/fintech-and-regtech-in-a-nutshell-and-the-future-in-a-sandbox

Financial Risk Tolerance: A Psychometric Review (June)

John E. Grable

This content provides financial analysts, investment professionals, and financial planners with a review of how financial risk-tolerance tests can and should be evaluated. It begins by clarifying terms related to risk taking, which is followed by a broad overview of two important measurement terms: validity and reliability. It concludes with examples for practice.

https://www.cfainstitute.org/en/research/foundation/2017/financial-risk-tolerance

Impact of Reporting Frequency on UK Public Companies (March)

Robert C. Pozen, Suresh Nallareddy, and Shivaram Rajgopal

Beginning in 2007, UK public companies were required to issue quarterly, rather than semiannual, financial reports. But the UK removed this quarterly reporting requirement in 2014. We studied the effects of these regulatory changes on UK public companies and found that the frequency of financial reports had no material impact on levels of corporate investment. However, mandatory quarterly reporting was associated with an increase in analyst coverage and an improvement in the accuracy of analyst earnings forecasts.

https://www.cfainstitute.org/en/research/foundation/2017/impact-of-reporting-frequency-on-uk-public-companies

2016

Monographs

Factor Investing and Asset Allocation: A Business Cycle Perspective (December)

Vasant Naik, Mukundan Devarajan, Andrew Nowobilski, Sébastien Page, CFA, and Niels Pedersen

This monograph draws heavily on the vast body of knowledge that has been built by financial economists over the last 50 years. Its goal is to show how to solve real-life portfolio allocation problems. We have found that using a broad range of models works best. Also, we prefer simple over complex models. We believe that simplicity and modularity lend substantial robustness to investment analysis. Importantly, the framework presented provides several of the "missing links" in asset allocation—for example, the links between asset classes and risk factors, between macroeconomic views and expected returns, and ultimately between quantitative and fundamental investing.

https://www.cfainstitute.org/en/research/foundation/2016/factor-investing-and-asset-allocation-a-business-cycle-perspective

Financial Market History: Reflections on the Past for Investors Today (December)

edited by David Chambers and Elroy Dimson

Since the 2008 financial crisis, a resurgence of interest in economic and financial history has occurred among investment professionals. This book discusses some of the lessons drawn from the past that may help practitioners when thinking about their portfolios. The book's editors, David Chambers and Elroy Dimson, are the academic leaders of the Newton Centre for Endowment Asset Management at the University of Cambridge in the United Kingdom.

https://www.cfainstitute.org/en/research/foundation/2016/financial-market-history

Let's All Learn How To Fish... To Sustain Long-Term Economic Growth (May)

Michael S. Falk, CFA

Today's economic growth challenges will become greater in the future because of the world's aging population, fertility trends and current levels, and current entitlement policies. Those challenges could be overcome, however, with thoughtful public policies and a culture that fosters responsibility and appreciation. This book reconsiders what makes us "healthy, wealthy, and wise." It focuses on how we might reimagine health care, retirement, and education policies to usher in a new ERA (from Entitlement to Responsibility with Appreciation) of sustainable long-term economic growth.

https://www.cfainstitute.org/en/research/foundation/2016/lets-all-learn-how-to-fish----to-sustain-long-term-economic-growth

Literature Reviews

"Technical Analysis: Modern Perspectives" (November)

Gordon Scott, CMT, Michael Carr, CMT, and Mark Cremonie, CMT, CFA

Supply and demand are cornerstones of economics, and the interaction of these forces is believed to explain price changes in all freely traded markets. Scarcity tends to result in increased prices, and abundance generally leads to lower prices. In financial markets, technical analysis provides a framework for informing investment management decisions by applying a supply and demand methodology to market prices. Technical analysts employ a disciplined, systematic approach that seeks to minimize the impact of behavioral biases and emotions that could adversely affect investment performance. Analysts employ ratio analysis, comparative analysis, and other techniques that are similar to the tools developed to analyze financial statements.

https://www.cfainstitute.org/en/research/foundation/2017/technical-analysis

Briefs

Gender Diversity in Investment Management: New Research for Practitioners on How to Close the Gender Gap (September)

Rebecca Fender, CFA, Renée Adams, Brad Barber, and Terrance Odean

We've completed the largest ever survey of investment management professionals on the subject of gender diversity.

https://www.cfainstitute.org/en/research/survey-reports/gender-diversity-report

Portfolio Structuring and the Value of Forecasting (August)

Jacques Lussier, CFA, Andrew Ang, PhD, Mark Carhart, CFA, Craig Bodenstab, CFA, Philip E. Tetlock, Warren Hatch, CFA, and David Rapach

Drawing from a CFA Montréal event, this analysis of factor investing reviews types of factors and risk premiums as well as the value of forecasting, including issues with accuracy and improving efficiency.

https://www.cfainstitute.org/en/research/foundation/2016/portfolio-structuring-and-the-value-of-forecasting

Overcoming the Notion of a Single Reference Currency: A Currency Basket Approach (April)

Giuseppe Ballocchi, CFA, and Hélie d'Hautefort

Wealthy families with a global footprint have liabilities and financial objectives in multiple currencies. To manage their currency risk, it is necessary to abandon the notion of a single reference currency in favor of a customized basket of currencies. We introduce the Global Reserve Currency Index, a useful proxy for the world currency.

https://www.cfainstitute.org/en/research/foundation/2016/overcoming-the-notion-of-a-single-reference-currency-a-currency-basket-approach

Annuities and Retirement Income Planning (February)

Patrick J. Collins, CFA

Annuitization is one asset management strategy for retirees seeking to secure lifetime income. The US annuity marketplace offers a variety of annuity contracts, including single premium annuities, advanced life deferred annuities, variable annuities with lifetime income guarantee riders, and ruin contingent deferred annuities. Advisers seeking to provide guidance to clients in or near retirement can benefit by understanding (1) the arguments both for and against annuitization and (2) how a client's interests might be best represented in the marketplace. Important annuity contract provisions are highlighted and briefly discussed so the adviser can become more familiar with retirement-planning options.

https://www.cfainstitute.org/en/research/foundation/2016/annuities-and-retirement-income-planning

Risk Profiling through a Behavioral Finance Lens (February)

Michael Pompian, CFA

This piece examines risk profiling through a behavioral finance lens. Advisers can classify clients into behavioral investor types to help determine what kind of investment plan they should recommend. With a better understanding of behavioral finance vis-à-vis risk taking, practitioners can enhance their understanding of client preferences and better inform their recommendations of investment strategies and products.

https://www.cfainstitute.org/en/research/foundation/2016/risk-profiling-through-a-behavioral-finance-lens

CFA Institute Research Foundation Board of Trustees

1 September 2018–31 August 2019

Chair
Ted Aronson, CFA
  AJO

Jeffery V. Bailey, CFA*
  Tonka Bay, MN

Bill Fung, PhD
  Aventura, FL

Diane Garnick
  Greenwich, CT

JT Grier, CFA*
  Virginia Retirement System

Joanne Hill
  CBOE Vest Financial

George R. Hoguet, CFA
  Chesham Investments, LLC

Robert Jenkins, FSIP
  London Business School

Joachim Klement, CFA
  Fidante Partners

Vikram Kuriyan, PhD, CFA
  GWA and Indian School of Business

Aaron Low, CFA
  LUMIQ

Diane Nordin, CFA
  Concord, MA

Mauro Miranda, CFA
  CFA Society Brazil

Sophie Palmer, CFA
  Jarislowsky Fraser

Paul Smith, CFA
  CFA Institute

*Emeritus

CFA Institute Research Foundation Board of Trustees

1 September 2019–31 August 2020

Chair
Ted Aronson, CFA
  AJO

Heather Brilliant, CFA
  Diamond Hill

Margaret Franklin, CFA
  CFA Institute

Bill Fung, PhD
  Aventura, FL

Daniel Gamba, CFA
  BlackRock

JT Grier, CFA*
  Virginia Retirement System

Joanne Hill
  CBOE Vest Financial

Roger Ibbotson*
  Yale School of Management

Joachim Klement, CFA
  Independent

Vikram Kuriyan, PhD, CFA
  GWA and Indian School of Business

Aaron Low, CFA
  LUMIQ

Mauro Miranda, CFA
  Panda Investimentos AAI Ltda.

Lotta Moberg, PhD, CFA
  William Blair

Sophie Palmer, CFA
  Jarislowsky Fraser

Dave Uduanu, CFA
  Sigma Pensions Ltd

*Emeritus

Officers and Directors

Executive Director
Bud Haslett, CFA
  CFA Institute

Gary P. Brinson Director of Research
Laurence B. Siegel
  Blue Moon Communications

Associate Research Director
Luis Garcia-Feijóo, CFA, CIPM
  Coral Gables, Florida

Secretary
Jessica Lawson
  CFA Institute

Treasurer
Kim Maynard
  CFA Institute

Made in the USA
Columbia, SC
20 November 2022

71530634R00046